The Strange Life of P.D. Ouspensky

By the same author:
ALEISTER CROWLEY: The Nature of the Beast
G.I. GURDJIEFF: The War Against Sleep
C.G. JUNG: Lord of the Underworld
RUDOLF STEINER: The Man and his Vision

The Strange Life of
P.D. OUSPENSKY

COLIN WILSON

Aquarian/Thorsons
An Imprint of HarperCollins*Publishers*

For Richard Foreman

The Aquarian Press
An Imprint of HarperCollins*Publishers*
77–85 Fulham Palace Road,
Hammersmith, London W6 8JB

Published by The Aquarian Press 1993
1 3 5 7 9 10 8 6 4 2

A catalogue record for this book
is available from the British Library

ISBN 1 85538 079 X

Typeset by Harper Phototypesetters Limited,
Northampton, England
Printed in Great Britain by
Mackays of Chatham, Kent, England

Contents

Foreword

A FEW hours before setting out for America in 1987, I casually picked up *A New Model of the Universe*, which happened to be lying by the bed because I had been duplicating the chapter on Time for a friend. I began to read 'Experimental Mysticism', and realized suddenly that this was the single most important chapter in all Ouspensky's work, and that what he was saying fitted closely with my own conclusions on the 'relationality' of consciousness, as outlined in the final chapter of my *Beyond the Occult*, which I had just finished. Oddly enough, I had read 'Experimental Mysticism' before – the chapter was heavily marked in pencil – yet, until that day, had never grasped its full significance. I duplicated it, took it with me to America, and used it as the basis of a number of lectures from New York to Los Angeles. On my return home I hastened to add sections on Ouspensky and 'Experimental Mysticism' to *Beyond the Occult*.

All this led me back to *Tertium Organum*, and to the recognition that even if he had never met Gurdjieff, Ouspensky would have been one of the most interesting thinkers of the twentieth century. This had, in fact, been the thesis of a book called *Ouspensky: The Unsung Genius* by J.H. Reyner. I had felt, at the time, that Reyner was pitching Ouspensky's claims too high; now I found myself feeling that, if anything, he had pitched them too low. Hence my own attempt in this book to stake Ouspensky's claim as an individual thinker and man of genius.

Acknowledgements

I WISH to thank Messrs Routledge and Kegan Paul for their permission to quote from the works of Ouspensky. Dr James Rentoul has drawn my attention to some interesting aspects of Ouspensky's work, as has Chloë Daly, of Laguna Beach, California.

I have dedicated this book to Richard Foreman – another student of the Work – in acknowledgement of the stimulus I received from his immense library while staying in his flat in New York.

CW, January 1992

One

The Dreamer

IN THE last years of his life, Ouspensky struck acquaintances as a sad and disappointed man; he drank too much, and spent a great deal of time brooding nostalgically about the good old days in Tsarist Russia. It was not entirely Slavic melancholy. He told J.G. Bennett in a letter that nothing could be found by intellectual processes, and that 'there is only one hope: that we should find the way to work with the higher emotional centre'. To this he added the sad comment: 'And we do not know how this is to be done.'

The disappointment may also have been due to a sense of creative unfulfilment. At the age of 20, he had made his reputation with a book called *The Fourth Dimension*. By the time he reached his mid-thirties – in 1913 – Ouspensky was one of the most promising young intellectuals in Russia, a fine novelist and writer of short stories, and the author of a brilliant and profound volume of philosophy called *Tertium Organum*. In fact when it was published in America after the First World War, it made him famous. His third book, *A New Model of the Universe*, was even finer, and guarantees him a place as one of the most important thinkers of the twentieth century. Ouspensky should have gone on to have become as well-known in the West as contemporaries like Berdyaev, Merejkovsky and Bunin. Instead, he descended into a self-chosen obscurity, preferring to regard himself as a teacher of 'the Work', the 'System' of his great contemporary George Ivanovich Gurdjieff. The latter achieved a considerable degree of celebrity in America during the 1930s. And Ouspensky, as far as he was known at all, was regarded simply as Gurdjieff's chief disciple – although, in fact, they had gone their separate ways soon after the First World War, and Ouspensky even forbade his pupils to mention Gurdjieff's name.

Ouspensky must have known that he was one of the most remarkable minds of the century – that he was no more a 'disciple' of Gurdjieff than, say, Coleridge was a disciple of Wordsworth, or Pushkin of Byron. No doubt he would have dismissed the whole question as an absurdity – fame, after all, is little more than a delusion – yet there is something in all of us that wishes to leave behind a name for posterity. And Ouspensky virtually renounced his own name and fame to become an anonymous teacher. Even those who revered him regarded him as a mouthpiece of Gurdjieff's ideas.

When he returned to England from New York in 1947, his former pupil Kenneth Walker was shocked by the change in him: '. . . he appeared to me to be a man who had lost all of his former enthusiasm and drive.' What was even more shocking was that Ouspensky had apparently lost faith in the System to which he had devoted his whole life. 'There is no System,' he replied in answer to a question. And so the sick man dragged himself on without faith for another nine months. His disciple Rodney Collin wrote: 'In Ouspensky's last months one saw how he accepted being old, sick, ugly, helpless, in pain, misunderstood . . .' And when, after a final talk to a small group of disciples, he died at dawn on 2 October, 1947, at the age of 69, Rodney Collin locked himself in Ouspensky's room for a week without food.

What had gone wrong? In fact, *had* anything gone wrong, or had Ouspensky brought his life's work to a kind of genuine fulfilment? To answer that question, we must go back to the beginning . . .

Pyotr Demianovich Ouspensky was born in Moscow on 5 March, 1878, the son of an officer in the Survey Service and a talented artist. Since in Russia one was either a peasant or a gentleman, Ouspensky was emphatically a gentleman. As his maternal grandparents were also members of the 'intelligentsia', he grew up among writers, artists and thinkers.

In a more stable society, he would undoubtedly have gone on to become one of the most important philosophers of his time and ended as a 'grand old man' whose name would have ranked with contemporaries like Bertrand Russell, Bernard Shaw and Thomas Mann.

Unfortunately, Holy Russia was one of the most unstable societies in the world. At the time of Ouspensky's birth, liberals were clamouring for a constitution. Organizations with titles like 'Land and Liberty' and 'The Will of the People' talked openly about revolution, and were persecuted by the police. Just after Ouspensky's third birthday, Tsar Alexander II was blown up by a bomb made of nitro-glycerine enclosed in glass. His successor, Alexander III, made a bizarre and heroic attempt to prevent Russia from advancing into the twentieth century by inaugurating a regime of repression, but died of exhaustion after a mere 13 years' rule. His successor, Nicholas II, 'the last of the Tsars', did his best to give the liberals the constitution they wanted, but it was too late: Russia was already living in the shadow of the immense tragedy that would engulf Europe and wipe out the Tsar's own family. In 1918, the year the Tsar and Tsarina were murdered at Ekaterinburg, Ouspensky set out on the journey that would take him into exile. The years of security were over and, at the age of 39, he had to start all over again.

Under the circumstances, it is not surprising that the young Ouspensky came to share the 'spirit of the age', and became imbued with a feverish romanticism; before he was seven, he was reading Turgenev's *Sportsman's Sketches* and Lermontov's *Hero of Our Time*, the latter a Byronic work by a poet who was killed in a duel at the age of 26. Both had been regarded as revolutionary works at the time of their publication and had earned their authors a period in prison.

Ouspensky's later description of memories of childhood – some dating from the age of two – indicate that, like the young Proust, he experienced life with an almost hallucinatory intensity. He spoke of the river near a town called Zvenigorod, with its smell of tar, its old monastery, and its hills covered with forests, and recalled the illuminations at the coronation of Tsar Alexander III, when he was three. Yet he also experienced a curious sense of the fundamental unreality of this world around him. He later told his pupils how, at the age of six, he had visited a place near Moscow (perhaps Zvenigorod) and thought that it was not as he remembered it from four years earlier. Then he realized that he had *not* been there before, and that his 'memory' of it must have been a dream.

He also told Kenneth Walker about the occasion when his mother took him to his first school. In a long corridor, when his mother admitted she was lost, Ouspensky told her that there was a passage further down, and that at the end of it there were two steps, and a window through which they would see the headmaster's garden, with lilies growing in it. The door of the headmaster's study was nearby. He proved to be correct, although he had never been in the building before.

This sense of the mystery and ambiguity of time continued to haunt his childhood; between the ages of six and eleven, he kept having experiences of *déjà vu* – 'I have been here before.' He and his young sister – to whom he was very close – shared an ability to foretell the immediate future: they would sit at the nursery window and predict – accurately – what would happen in the street. They never spoke to the adults about this, convinced that they wouldn't understand anyway.

Nevertheless, Ouspensky was fortunate in his parents. Through his mother he came to love poetry and the visual arts. But his father was also a keen amateur mathematician, who was fascinated by the then-fashionable subject of the fourth dimension, and by the age of 12, Ouspensky was as interested in science as in literature and art. The Latin master who caught him reading a physics textbook in class confiscated it, and his fellow pupils murmured mockingly that Ouspensky read physics. From the autobiographical novel *The Strange Life of Ivan Osokin* – started when he was in his mid-twenties – we gather that he had a particular dislike of this master, a German, and that he was generally a rebellious pupil.

Osokin is, in fact, our main source of information about Ouspensky's childhood and teens. It is a novel about 'Eternal Recurrence', in which the hero, on the verge of committing suicide because he has lost the girl he loves, goes to see a magician, who offers to allow him to live the past few years over again. But it makes no difference; he makes all the same mistakes, loses the girl again, and once more goes to see the magician, to ask to be allowed to live his life over again . . .

How can we be sure that *Osokin* is autobiographical? Because Ouspensky admitted that the girl, Zinaida, was a real person, and we know that certain other events in the novel also happened to him – for example, that he was expelled from school for a silly practical joke, that his mother died within two years of his expulsion, and that he went to Paris. His portrait of the rebellious young Osokin is also close to what Ouspensky tells us about himself elsewhere. Like Osokin, Ouspensky was a boarder at the Second Moscow Gymnasium; like Osokin, he found the place stifling and squalid. 'I often want to smash my head against the wall from sheer boredom.' His neglect of his studies led the headmaster to order him to stay behind after school one day. Osokin finds that the caretaker has forgotten to lock him in. He walks along the corridor, adorns a bust of Julius Caesar with a pair of blue spectacles, and writes on the wall underneath it 'Welcome your Excellency' – his Excellency being a school inspector who was expected later in the day. The next day he is expelled.

Ouspensky's own expulsion – at the age of 16 – seems to have done him no harm. He enrolled as a 'free listener' at Moscow University, and completed his education by reading. He was an excellent linguist, who had already learned English (although he never learned to speak it without a strong Russian accent), and in the 18 months after leaving school learned Italian well enough to read Dante. But a deep distaste for Latin and Greek prevented him from going on to take a degree. In the year he left school he discovered Nietzsche, and was deeply struck by his concept of Eternal Recurrence. This, Ouspensky concluded, was what he had experienced in childhood – the moods of 'I have been here before.'

A year later, his mother died. Perhaps to recover from the shock, Ouspensky began to travel – to Paris and to remote parts of Russia. In *Osokin*, he describes a visit to an uncle who lives on his country estate, and a love affair with his uncle's ward Tanechka (a diminutive of Tania). The girl is two years Osokin's senior. They flirt, kiss and go for long walks in the woods. He is covered with embarrassment when she calls him and he finds her standing naked in a stream. After that she spends the night in his room – it seems clear that she is the one who does the seducing. Osokin's uncle finds out and sends him back to Moscow to become a student at the military academy. As far as we know, Ouspensky was never at a military academy – but information about his early years is so sparse that he may well have been. What we *do* know is that he attended parties, drank too much vodka and was known to every policeman in Moscow because, far from being quarrelsome when drunk, he tried to act as peacemaker. 'One night,' he told Carl Bechhofer Roberts, 'I remember I got home with the left sleeve of my overcoat missing. How I lost it, and where, I have never discovered.' Apart from such glimpses, we have virtually no idea of what Ouspensky did during the 10 years between his expulsion from school and 1905, when his affair with Zinaida came to an end and he tried to exorcise his misery by writing *Ivan Osokin* (originally entitled 'The Wheel of Fortune') as a kind of film outline.

This was also the year of the abortive revolution, when troops fired upon peaceable crowds who had marched to the Winter Palace to present a petition to the Tsar. In the past 20 years, Russia had become increasingly ungovernable, and the new Tsar, Nicholas II, was a vacillator who changed his mind every day or so. He could not decide whether to establish a military dictatorship or to give the liberals the constitution they wanted. Finally, he gave a constitution with one hand and took it back with the other: that is, he allowed the people to elect a parliament (called the Duma), but still kept his own government, which held all the real power. He was determined to remain an absolute ruler, but lacked all the necessary qualities. He was a weakling and a dreamer, who preferred to spend his days in his summer palace with his family rather than getting on with the business of running the country and trying to avert the revolution prophesied by the anarchists and Marxists.

Ouspensky's beloved younger sister (we do not even have a record of her name) was also a dreamer and, like so many idealistic students, she joined the revolutionary movement. She was among those arrested in 1905 and thrown into prison. Her arrest must have been a tragedy for Ouspensky, who would have recalled clearly the fate of another idealistic student, Marie Vietroff, who had been confined in the Peter and Paul fortress in 1896 because a forbidden book had been found in her room, and who had committed suicide by burning herself to death after months of ill treatment, including rape. When, in 1908, Ouspensky's sister died in prison, it must have confirmed his feeling that life is basically futile and tragic.

The truth is that Ouspensky, like the Tsar, was basically an ineffectual dreamer and a weakling. This is something that his later disciples would have found hard to imagine, for they knew him as a hard, stern man who was impatient of all talk of mysticism, and whose squarely-built figure seemed to reflect his pragmatic disposition. But we only have to consider the facts to see that this is not a true picture. After being expelled from school – which he hated with the ardour of a romantic who regards boredom as an affront to his dignity – he failed to keep his promise to take a degree and spent his legacy wandering ineffectually from place to place, vaguely seeking for something he could not define. He later claimed that he was 'never such a fool' as Osokin, but this is hard to believe. In fact, what *Osokin* reveals is a dangerously romantic young man who is immensely susceptible to women – Tanechka, Anna, Loulou, Valerie, Zinaida – and who seems to believe that if only he could find the right one all his problems would disappear . . .

Most young Russians in Ouspensky's position would have found a job in the civil service – which required very little effort – and devoted themselves to the struggle for

achievement in other spheres. Ouspensky merely seems to
have wasted his legacy (Osokin gambles it away), so that by
1905, when he was 27, he had to start making a living by
journalism. In *A New Model of the Universe*, he offers us a
glimpse of himself in 1906 or 1907, sitting in the editorial office
of the Moscow newspaper *The Morning*, trying to read foreign
newspapers in French, German, English and Italian in order
to write an article on the forthcoming Hague Conference:

> Phrases, phrases, sympathetic, critical, ironical, blatant,
> pompous, lying, and, worst of all, utterly automatic phrases
> . . . But what can I say? It is all so tedious. Diplomats and all
> kinds of statesmen will gather together and talk, papers will
> approve or disapprove, sympathise or not sympathise. Then
> everything will be as it was, or even worse.

And so he pushes aside the newspapers and opens a drawer
of his desk 'crammed with books with titles like *The Occult
World, Life after Death, Atlantis and Lemuria, Dogme et Rituel de
la Haute Magie, Le Temple de Satan* and the like . . . I open
one of the books, feeling that my article will not be written
today . . .'

This is fundamentally the nostalgic romanticism of the
1890s, of Dowson and Verlaine drinking themselves to death
on absinthe, of W.B. Yeats daydreaming of fairyland because
he detests the real world. It is also the attitude of Goncharov's
Oblomov, unable to arouse himself to get out of bed, and of
Gogol's landowner Manilov, whose fantasies of fame and
fortune 'grew so lively that eventually he could not even
follow them himself'. Amusingly enough, Ouspensky
compares the Hague peacemakers to Gogol's Manilov – a
classic example of the pot calling the kettle black.

Ouspensky goes on to meditate that he would like to print
his true thoughts about the Hague Conference, but knows
that they would only land him in jail. And even if they got
into print, nobody would read them. 'What is the use of
attempting to expose lies when people like them and live by
them? It is their own affair; but I am tired of lying . . .' And

so he turns back to his books on magic and Atlantis . . . All of which makes it very clear that even in his late twenties, Ouspensky was still a rather ineffectual romantic who blamed the world for his own shortcomings.

We know little of these years except that Ouspensky attended meetings of the Theosophical Society and travelled widely as a journalist. In his introduction to a translation of Ouspensky's *Talks with a Devil*, J.G. Bennett writes:

> Little is known of this period of his life, and I can report only the episodes I heard from him in the course of conversations. He was a successful journalist working on the leading Russian papers, but more often as a free lance. He travelled in Europe and the United States writing articles for St Petersburg papers between 1908 and 1912.

(St Petersburg may here be a slip for Moscow.)

It was in 1912 that Ouspensky achieved his ambition to go to India with an open commission to write articles for three Russian newspapers. He proceeded via London, and there made an acquaintance who later proved to be extremely valuable – A.R. Orage, a charismatic socialist who was the editor of one of the most widely read magazines of the period, *The New Age*. Promising Orage to send him some contributions, Ouspensky then travelled on to Egypt, where he was deeply fascinated by the Sphinx, then to India, where he met some of the outstanding yogis of his time, including Aurobindo. He was not impressed by any of them. He explained afterwards that he was looking for 'real knowledge' and had found only holy men who may have achieved liberation for themselves but could not transmit their methods to others. He also spent some time at Adhyar in Madras, the headquarters of the Theosophical Society, of which he had been a member since 1906. In later years he liked to tell the story of the 'caste system' at Adhyar. On the ground floor were all the hangers-on and undistinguished visitors. The second floor was reserved for well-wishers who gave their money and support to the society. The top floor, with a large open roof, was the home of the esoteric group, the real initiates of Theosophy. Ouspensky recalled with relish that he was at once admitted to the esoteric group in spite of his no longer being a member of the Theosophical Society and his open criticism of their founder, Helena Blavatsky. He asserted that he found nothing at Adhyar that made him wish to stay. According to J.G. Bennett:

> He went on to Ceylon, which he found more congenial, and he met several of the more famous *bhikkus*, and satisfied himself that the old techniques of Buddhism were still being used in Ceylon. But once again he felt no urge to cut himself off from the West and become a monk. He wrote later that he was not interested in a way that would isolate him from the Western world, which held the key to the future of mankind. This did not mean that he doubted the existence of 'schools', as he called them, in India and Ceylon, but that these schools no longer had the significance that they used to have in the past. He also added that he found that most of these schools relied upon religious and devotional techniques that he was convinced were insufficient for penetrating into the essential reality for which he was seeking.

No doubt full records of this period of Ouspensky's life exist in the various newspapers he wrote for and will one day be published by some diligent researcher. Yet, while they would provide us with facts, they could hardly help us to a deeper understanding than Ouspensky himself provides in *Osokin* and the slightly later *Talks with a Devil*.

The latter consists of two stories, the first of which, 'The Inventor', utilizes Ouspensky's American experience. The inventor is an American called Hugh B., who finds himself working in a factory, at a job that bores him. One day, as he is copying a design for a new machine, he realizes that it could be improved by a simple change. The designer becomes indignant at the suggestion and shouts at him. But the manager begins to see that Hugh is correct, and makes him senior draughtsman. Hugh is still dissatisfied because he is still underpaid for his inventions. He marries, but he and his wife are soon at loggerheads. All his attempts to achieve recognition as an inventor come to nothing. One day, like Ivan Osokin, he decides to commit suicide . . .

But at this point, fate intervenes to change his life. As he is buying a revolver with which to end his life, he has an idea for an automatic revolver that will fire like a machine gun. By the time he gets back home, his wife has left him, but he is so obsessed by his new invention that he takes it in his stride. (At this point, the devil who is recounting the story to Ouspensky has to admit that he cannot even begin to understand how a man can become enthusiastic about a mere invention . . .)

The prototype revolver is made, but no one seems to be interested. When one day Hugh encounters another inventor whose life has been a total failure, he almost loses courage. But eventually he meets a friend who is about to sell his factory, and the two go into partnership. At last, the new revolver is manufactured – but it sells so badly that Hugh is tempted to dispose of his patent for 1,000 dollars . . .

At this point, though, fate again takes a hand. In Paris, a famous singer is murdered by her lesbian lover with one of Hugh's revolvers. A book about the case becomes a bestseller and Hugh's factory is suddenly inundated with orders. Every time there is a murder or political catastrophe involving the new repeating pistol, they receive still more orders. Soon Hugh is a millionaire and is reunited with his wife . . .

So far, the story seems to be as deeply pessimistic as *Osokin*: despair leads to the decision to commit suicide; fate intervenes and brings success, but the success involves death and misery, and the death and misery bring still more success until the inventor feels that life has become meaningless. But at this point, we become aware that Ouspensky is no longer a pessimist trapped in the idea of Eternal Recurrence. As Hugh stands on the bridge of his yacht on the Amazon, gazing at the stars, he is suddenly imbued with a passion for astronomy. He spends the rest of the cruise reading books about the stars and, when he returns home, builds an observatory. 'Now he worked for the sake of knowledge alone, creative work, winning over and extorting from nature her closest secrets . . .' Hugh has slipped out of the grip of the devil, whose aim is to confine human beings to the narrowness of the material world. And when his wife decides to devote herself to healing the blind, the devil takes his leave, protesting that he is revolted by her sentimentality.

In a footnote in *Talks with a Devil*, Ouspensky acknowledges that he has unconsciously plagiarized an idea from Dostoevsky's scene with the Devil in *The Brothers Karamazov*. In fact, *Talks with a Devil* is altogether closer to the third act of Shaw's *Man and Superman*, the dream episode called 'Don Juan in Hell'. Shaw's Devil is also a materialist, who has designed Hell as a place where human beings can relax and enjoy themselves. He believes that the aim of life is happiness, good fellowship and artistic enjoyment. Understandably, religious people strike him as cranks; so do philosophers and scientists and all human beings driven by an obscure craving to evolve. Shaw argues that the purpose of the 'Life Force' is to create Intelligence, a brain through which Life can become conscious of its own purposes, so that it can pursue these purposes in the full light of consciousness. Nothing can satisfy the highest type of human being except to help life in its struggle to evolve.

In the second of the *Talks with a Devil*, the story called 'The Benevolent Devil', Ouspensky develops ideas that are strikingly similar to Shaw's. He describes a visit to the caves of Ellora, in Northeast Bombay state, which is followed by a dream in which he meets the Devil (now spelt with a capital D) in the temple of Kailas, and they resume the conversation that was broken off in the previous story.

The Devil begins by explaining that, as far as he is concerned, 'this' world is the only reality, and there is nothing beyond it. 'The kingdom of matter is eternal.' Then he explains that there are two kinds of human beings: one, the descendants of animals, who live entirely on the material plane, and 'whose lives consist of harbouring grudges and trying to get out of difficulties by burdening others with them', and two, the descendants of Adam and Eve, who suffer from 'religious mania', and believe in absurd ideals. He goes on to explain how he seduced Adam and Eve into materialism by giving them large quantities of a delicious fruit which they liked so much that they began to eat it three times a day. They became so obsessed by this fruit that they forgot all their 'imaginary ideals'. Then they began to quarrel, and when Eve left Adam, he found himself three wives from a nearby tribe, while Eve took a lover. And so the Fall began . . .

Unfortunately, the descendants of Adam and Eve have never lost their vision of the imaginary ideal and it takes a whole army of devils to prevent them from backsliding into virtue.

The Devil now tells the story of a young man called Leslie White, to whom Ouspensky has introduced a Sinhalese yogi. After a long talk with the yogi, Leslie decides to forgo his dinner – he is not really hungry anyway – and to spend the evening reading some books that have arrived that morning. Watched anxiously by his personal little demon, Leslie settles down in an armchair with a weak whisky and soda. As soon as he becomes absorbed in the world of the books, the demon loses sight of him; Leslie seems to vanish into thin air. This, Ouspensky realizes, is because 'his whole being was immersed in the world of ideas, and material reality did not exist for him'.

> So that is the secret, I thought. To get away from reality means to get away from the devil, to become invisible to him. This . . . signifies, in reverse, that people of dull reality, practical, workaday people, in general all ordinary sober people, belong absolutely and completely to the devil . . . To be frank, I was delighted by this discovery.

Love, it seems, is another way in which the demon can 'lose' his prey, for when a person is romantically in love, the feeling surrounds him like a wall, and he becomes invisible . . .

The demon servant now begins trying to seduce Leslie back to laziness and self-indulgence. To dull his senses, he puts him out an unusually large and tasty breakfast. Leslie is unable to resist it and his sense of latent possibilities collapses . . .

Later that day he goes to tea at the house of Lady Gerald, and there he sees, for the second time, a girl called Margaret, to whom he is powerfully attracted. She obviously feels the same. He begins to tell her about the old yogi and she understands him.

> Leslie suddenly understood that if he could take the two steps which separated him from Margaret and then take her by the waist and lead her right down to the sea, walk with her along the water's edge, feel it roll under their feet, further and further on, until the stars began to shine, somewhere where there were no people, but only the two of them, then straightaway everything that the old Indian had spoken about would become a complete reality.

But the moment passes – and as it does so, Leslie has an overwhelming sense that this has all happened before, and that he has lost Margaret before in the same way.

On his way home, he daydreams about her, and again the demon feels he is losing him. So he sends someone to invite him to dinner, and then makes sure that he overeats. (The demon can even turn himself into particularly delicious-looking dishes.) Finally, although tempted to stay awake and think out his problems, Leslie has a whisky and soda, and falls asleep. The demon looks utterly exhausted.

> 'You see,' said the Devil, 'that is what our life is like. Is that not self-sacrifice? Think of it: the poor little devil must keep watch over every step he takes, not leaving him even for one moment. He allows himself to be eaten up, works himself into such a state, and there is still the risk of losing him because of his various silly fantasies . . .'

And it seems that Leslie is, in fact, lost to his demon. The words of the yogi have awakened him, and he goes into a Buddhist monastery and begins to practise fasting and meditation. 'But,' says the Devil, 'I have not lost him yet. I still have one trick up my sleeve. The stake is on nobility . . .'

Ouspensky learns what he means when he sees Leslie again in London, two months after the outbreak of the First World War. He is marching alongside his platoon, on his way to fight. 'The stake is on nobility . . .' War, in which the descendants of Adam and Eve fight one another and believe it is all for the sake of the highest ideals, is the Devil's ultimate seduction . . . This time the Devil has won.

Together with *Ivan Osokin*, these two *Talks with a Devil* afford a fundamental insight into Ouspensky's vision of human existence. It is at once romantic and pessimistic. The world is divided into black and white: the children of Adam and the descendants of the beasts, who belong to the Devil. Daydreaming enables us to escape from the Devil. So does falling in love. But the Devil usually has an extra trick up his sleeve, and man's chances of evolving are very slim indeed.

It never seems to strike Ouspensky that daydreaming, and the kind of lassitude and pessimism that can spring from it, are as harmful in their way as the Devil's materialism. They encourage man to sit on the sidelines and sneer at the peacemakers while escaping into a world of romantic imaginings. They encourage him to believe that the answer lies in finding an ideal woman, or in finding a Teacher who can initiate him into the Great Secret. In short, they encourage him to look everywhere for the answer but inside himself . . .

Yet all this is not entirely fair to Ouspensky. For by 1914 – when he was on the eve of meeting his long-awaited Teacher – he had already taken some major steps towards solving the problems that tormented Ivan Osokin. In fact, in some respects he had even gone further than his Teacher.

Two

The Romantic Realist

OUSPENSKY SAILED from London, and arrived back in a St Petersburg whose name had been changed to Petrograd (because in the frenzy of World War One patriotism, St Petersburg sounded too German).

Back in his newspaper office in Moscow, he saw a notice for a ballet called *The Struggle of the Magicians*, which declared that the action took place in India and would give a complete picture of Oriental magic. Ouspensky published it in his column, with the sarcastic comment that it would contain everything that cannot be found in the real India. After that, he went to Petrograd, where he delivered two highly successful lectures about his travels in the East, both of which attracted audiences of more than a thousand.

It was when he repeated the same lectures in Moscow that two new acquaintances – a musician and a sculptor – told him about a teacher called Gurdjieff, a Caucasian Greek who was also the author of the ballet about India. It seemed that Gurdjieff possessed remarkable hypnotic powers. Ouspensky was sceptical: 'People invent miracles for themselves, and invent exactly what is expected from them.' Nevertheless, he eventually agreed to meet Gurdjieff.

We arrived in a small café in a noisy though not central street. I saw a man of an oriental type, no longer young, with a black moustache and piercing eyes, who astonished me first of all because he seemed to be . . . completely out of keeping with the place and its atmosphere . . . this man, with the face of an Indian rajah or an Arab sheik, whom I at once seemed to see

in a white burnoose or a gilded turban . . . produced the . . .
impression of a man poorly disguised.

Gurdjieff spoke with a strong Caucasian accent, which would
have sounded rather provincial to Ouspensky.

And what did Gurdjieff see? Ouspensky was a man of
medium height, with closely cropped hair, a prim mouth, and
eyes that peered short-sightedly through thick pince-nez
glasses. Another disciple of Gurdjieff, the musician Thomas
de Hartmann, described him as 'simple, courteous,
approachable and intelligent'. In later years he struck people
as unapproachable and cold; in March 1915, he would still
have been a great deal like the romantic young student who
got drunk on vodka and tried to make peace with everybody.
But he was also a well-known writer and journalist, whose
lectures had attracted widespread attention; so he now had
the confidence not to succumb to the charisma of this man
with the piercing eyes, but to regard him with a certain
scepticism. And although Gurdjieff spoke knowledgeably
about yoga, Ouspensky's scepticism seemed to be justified
when Gurdjieff declined to name some of the eminent
professors whom he claimed were interested in his work. It
increased when Gurdjieff took him to a flat to meet his pupils.
He had spoken of the enormous expense of the apartments
he had taken for his 'Work', but this place was obviously the
kind of flat that schoolteachers were given free. One of the
pupils read aloud from a manuscript in which someone
described a meeting with Gurdjieff; it struck Ouspensky as
obscure and lacking in literary skill. When Gurdjieff asked
him if it could be published in a newspaper, Ouspensky
suspected that this oriental gentleman was simply trying to
make use of him. As he left the place – in company with one
of the pupils – Ouspensky was tempted to make fun of
Gurdjieff, but allowed caution to prevail.

In fact, as he discovered later, Gurdjieff made a habit of
trying to present himself in the worst possible light when he
first met potential pupils. If they assumed he was a charlatan,
it proved they lacked penetration. Ouspensky was not put off;

he accepted subsequent suggestions to meet Gurdjieff in noisy cafés, and was not even discouraged when Gurdjieff suggested that he should pay 1,000 roubles a year. But when Gurdjieff hinted that he was willing to accept Ouspensky as a pupil, Ouspensky explained that he would be unable to give any undertaking to keep Gurdjieff's teachings secret. Gurdjieff apparently acceded to this. 'There are no conditions of any kind . . . Our starting point is that man does not know himself, that he is *not*.' He went on to state the principle that Ouspensky was to emphasize for the rest of his life: that man has no single 'I', but dozens of 'I's', replacing one another with the bewildering rapidity of a game of musical chairs. And at a later meeting, he stated his basic principle: that human beings are basically *machines*, and that our belief that we possess free will is an illusion. Man *could* develop some degree of free will, but it would cost an immense effort. Moreover, his starting point would need to be the recognition that he is basically a machine, a kind of robot, merely reacting to stimuli like a penny-in-the-slot machine.

Ouspensky was deeply impressed. All this was very close to his own feelings about human beings, the feelings he had expressed in *Osokin* and 'The Inventor'. But in 'The Inventor', he had made the assumption that his hero could escape from 'the trap' by turning his attention to higher intellectual pursuits. If Gurdjieff was correct, that would do him no good whatsoever; an intellectual is as 'robotic' as a peasant.

> 'Take yourself,' said Gurdjieff. 'If you understood everything you had written in your own book, what is it called?' – he made something impossible out of the words 'Tertium Organum' – 'I should come and bow down to you and beg you to teach me. But *you do not understand* either what you read or what you write.'

It was a disturbing picture – even more disturbing than Ouspensky's own picture of man as a plaything of demons, or a helpless puppet in the grip of Eternal Recurrence. Yet apparently Gurdjieff was certain that there *was* an escape from the trap. Man *could* be galvanized out of his condition of 'sleep' into something like waking consciousness. It was this assurance that led Ouspensky to decide to accept Gurdjieff as his teacher.

This was, of course, inevitable. Ouspensky had spent so many years looking for someone to tell him 'The Answer', how to achieve 'higher states' of awareness, how to hold on to the mystical glimpses of sheer affirmation, that if he had decided to ignore Gurdjieff's offer, he would have spent the rest of his life wondering what he had missed. Yet with the wisdom of hindsight, we can see that his decision involved certain disadvantages that would continue to haunt him for the rest of his life. Gurdjieff was right when he said that if Ouspensky had understood everything he had written in *Tertium Organum*, he would have been a great teacher. In spite of the pessimism of *Osokin* and *Talks with a Devil*, Ouspensky had come very close indeed to finding his own answer. There was a basic sense in which he did not need Gurdjieff. In order to understand this, we need to look more closely at *Tertium Organum* (subtitled 'A Key to the Enigmas of the World'), which had been published in 1912.

Let us begin by looking at an experience that dated from 1908:

It was in the sea of Marmora, on a rainy day of winter, the far-off high and rocky shores were of a pronounced violet colour of every shade, including the most tender, fading into grey and blending with the grey sky. The sea was the colour of lead mixed with silver. I remember all these colours. The steamer was going north. I remained at the rail, looking at the waves. The white crest of waves were running towards us. A wave would run at the ship, raised as if desiring to hurl its crest upon it, rushing up with a howl. The steamer heeled, shuddered and slowly straightened back; then from afar a new wave came running. I watched this play of waves with the ship, and felt them draw me to themselves. It was not at all that desire to jump down which one feels in mountains but something infinitely more subtle. The waves were drawing my soul to themselves. And suddenly I felt that it went to them. It lasted an instant, perhaps less than an instant, but I entered into the waves, and with them rushed with a howl at the ship. And in that instant *I became all*. The waves – they were myself; the far violet mountains, the wind, the clouds hurrying from the north, the great steamship, heeling and rushing irresistibly forward – all were myself. I sensed the enormous heavy body – my body – all its motions, shudderings, waverings and vibrations, fire, pressure of steam and weight of engines were *inside* me, the unmerciful and unyielding propelling screw which pushed and pushed me forward, never for a moment releasing me, the rudder which determined all my motion – all this was myself: also two sailors . . . and the black snake of smoke coming in clouds out of the funnel . . . all.

It was an instant of unusual freedom, joy and expansion. A second – and the spell of the charm disappeared. It passed like a dream when one tries to remember it. But the sensation was so powerful, so bright and so unusual that I was afraid to move and waited for it to recur. But it did not return, and a moment later I could not say that it had been – could not say whether it was a reality or merely the *thought* that, looking at the waves, it might be so.

Two years later, the yellowish waves of the Finnish gulf and a green sky gave me a taste of the same sensation, but this time it was dissipated almost before it appeared.

Now what has happened to Ouspensky is very clear. The sheer exhilaration of the waves has momentarily lifted his consciousness into an orgasmic sensation of sheer power, enormous health and strength. Our senses normally seem to extend scarcely beyond our bodies; objects seen around us are dim and slightly unreal. But a sudden great effort of will, or a *reflection* of the external forces of nature, can strengthen the 'intentionality' of perception so that our gaze seems to be a spear thrown from behind the eyes. In such moments, our usual vapid, feeble sense of our own identity vanishes for a moment in a sense of sheer joy. Hence the feeling of 'oneness'. It could be compared to the sensation one might experience if, in a crowd cheering with happiness, one flung one's arms around a total stranger and felt as much love as for one's brother or sister.

This is basically the 'secret' Ouspensky was looking for. Since he was personally so withdrawn and shy, it must have seemed beyond his grasp. But the sensation his experience left behind was obviously that *our senses act as jailers*, preventing us from grasping the reality that lies around us.

This leads us to the starting point of *Tertium Organum*, a chapter called (rather unpromisingly) 'Subjective and Objective'. What, Ouspensky asks, do we really know about that world 'outside' us? If he could feel that he had *become* the waves and the ship, how can the usual distinction between subject and object be as 'real' as it seems?

According to Bishop Berkeley, such a distinction *is* quite unreal. Our senses are not 'windows'; they are *interpreters*, and they *translate* the information that bombards them into terms we can understand. Energy of 16 millionths of an inch strikes our eyes, and our eyes translate it into redness. Energy of 32 millionths of an inch strikes us, and we translate it into violet. Energy of a higher wavelength – ultra-violet, for example – is invisible to us because our senses feel that it is of no use to us. So we do not live in a real world, but in an interpreted world. That tree is 'out there', but for all practical purposes it is inside my head. Berkeley argues that we have no *proof* of the existence of a world 'out there'; it might all be a delusion, like a film show projected on my eyeballs.

Kant did his best to rescue philosophy from this uncomfortable position. We do not *create* the real world, he says, but our senses *establish the conditions* for the world we see. They are rather like a nightclub doorkeeper who will only let in people who are respectably dressed. And their criterion for respectability, says Kant, is that things have to be dressed in *space and time*. Nakedness is not allowed.

But this means that you and I can never know what the clients look like without their clothes on. We can never know the 'things in themselves', as they were before they had to put on dinner jackets and long dresses. So, at any rate, said Kant. And Ouspensky is willing to accept his views on the matter.

But in the last decades of the nineteenth century, a writer called C.H. Hinton caused a sensation by extending Kant's idea in a most fascinating manner. Very well, says Hinton, our senses act like doorkeepers who force the clientele to dress in a respectable manner. But in that case, it is our senses that make the rule that our world has three dimensions – length, breadth and height. Why should it not relax its standards, and permit a world with *four* dimensions – length, breadth, height, and another dimension at right angles to these?

Why make such a supposition in the first place? It seems to have come about as a result of some of the puzzles of the new 'science' of psychical research, which began to come into being in the 1860s. The 'occult revival' began in 1848, with loud banging and rapping noises in the house of a New York farmer named Fox. These later turned into classic 'poltergeist' phenomena, with objects flying through the air. Soon hundreds of 'mediums' were causing even more spectacular effects – trumpets played themselves as they floated in space, tables rose from the ground, flowers materialized out of the air, and ghostly hands stroked the faces of the 'sitters' at séances. Moreover, poltergeists seemed to have the ability to cause solid objects to fly through walls. The solution, many 'Spiritualists' came to believe, was a fourth dimension. If spirits inhabited a universe with an extra dimension, then a poltergeist would not actually be throwing an object through a wall, but 'over' it, into the fourth dimension – just as a giant could step over a wall that would be an insurmountable obstacle to a beetle.

A Professor Johann Carl Friederich Zollner, of the University of Leipzig, seems to have originated this theory that spirits inhabit a four-dimensional world, and he decided to test it by asking a 'medium' if he could get the spirits to tie a knot in a piece of string whose two ends had been joined together in a circle (and also sealed with sealing wax). The experiment took place in 1877, with an American medium called Henry Slade, and Slade – or the spirits – tied the knot in the string at his first attempt. One of the witnesses to the experiment was Zollner's fellow professor Gustav Fechner, who had written an essay on 'Why Space Has Four Dimensions' as early as 1846. Unfortunately, Slade had been tried and convicted of cheating in London in the previous year – Professor Ray Lankester had snatched a slate before the 'spirits' had time to write on it, and found that it was already written on. Slade insisted that he had heard the squeak of the slate pencil moments before Lankester snatched the slate.

Alas, in later life, Slade was often caught cheating, which would seem to dispose of him as a witness for the fourth dimension. But this assumption may be too hasty. The Society for Psychical Research, formed in 1882, reached the conclusion that although mediums *do* cheat, the evidence for the reality of spiritualistic phenomena – including poltergeists – is overwhelming. Their experience also confirmed that many 'genuine' mediums sometimes resorted to cheating. Slade was later caught cheating before the Seybert Committee in Philadelphia, and he acknowledged to them that Zollner had watched him closely only for the first three or four sittings, then allowed him to do as he liked. But since the knotted string was produced at the first sitting, it seems possible that it was genuine.

To Ouspensky, it seemed obvious that the idea of the fourth dimension is one of the most important that human beings can contemplate. When we are tired, our minds simply accept the material world around us without question; everything is merely 'itself'. But as soon as we experience the sense of happiness and excitement that often comes on spring mornings, or setting out on holiday, the world is seen to be full of infinite possibilities, and nothing is merely 'itself': everything seems to *stand for something* that is more than itself, just as the words on this page stand for something more than themselves. Hinton himself grasped this notion in an essay called 'Many Dimensions', where he speaks of errand boys reading 'penny dreadfuls', and how they could be spending their time more fruitfully 'communing with space' (which for Hinton meant trying to think three-dimensionally). Then he goes on to say:

And yet, looking at the same printed papers, being curious and looking deeper and deeper into them with a microscope, I have seen that in splodgy ink stroke and dull fibrous texture, each part was definite, exact, absolutely so far and no farther, punctiliously correct; and deeper and deeper lying a wealth of form, a rich variety and amplitude of shapes, that in a moment leapt higher than my wildest dreams could conceive.

What Hinton means is that the paper contains all the mysteries of space itself. But he might have gone farther, and recognized that even the silliest penny dreadful, explored to its depths, would reveal unknown vistas of the human imagination.

This is the aspect of the fourth dimension that fascinates Ouspensky. And he expands it in some of the most remarkable and profound pages of *Tertium Organum*. Chapter 14 begins:

> It seems to us that we see something and understand something. But in reality all that proceeds around us we sense only very confusedly, just as a snail senses confusedly the sunlight, the darkness and the rain.

Here we note immediately the quality that makes Ouspensky such a good writer: his clarity. He has an enviable ability to say exactly and precisely what he means. But this image of the snail does more than that: it conveys in a few words Ouspensky's feeling that we are surrounded by a vast, unknown universe, and that our *assumptions and presuppositions* cut us off from this world of reality. We may, in fact, reject Kant, and his notion that space and time are merely the clothes that the nightclub doorman forces the customers to wear; we may even assume that that pillar box really is red, and not that our eyes merely interpret its wavelength as redness. But we may nevertheless accept Ouspensky's central point: that our perception is 'prejudiced', and we often see only what we expect to see.

Ouspensky goes on to tell a story that makes the same point. He describes how he and a friend were crossing the River Neva in St Petersburg:

We had been talking, but both fell silent as we approached the [Peter and Paul] fortress, gazing up at its walls and making probably the same reflection. 'Right there are also factory chimneys,' said A. Behind the walls of the fortress indeed appeared some brick chimneys blackened by smoke.

On his saying this, I too sensed the *difference between* the chimneys and the prison walls with *unusual clearness* and like an electric shock. I realised *the difference between the very bricks themselves* . . .

Later in conversation with A, I recalled this episode, and he told me that not only then, but *always*, he sensed these differences and was deeply convinced of their reality.

Ouspensky goes on to say that the wood of a gallows, a crucifix and the mast of a ship is, in fact, a *quite different material* in each case. Chemical analysis could not detect it; but then, chemical analysis cannot detect the difference between twins, who are nevertheless quite different personalities.

They are only the *shadows* of real things, *the substance of which is contained in their function*. The shadow of a sailor, of a hangman and of an ascetic may be quite similar – it is impossible to distinguish them by their shadows, just as it is impossible to find any difference between the wood of a mast, of a gallows and of a cross by chemical analysis.

This realization is an extension of his insight on the Sea of Marmora. In that case, sheer exaltation had somehow amplified the strength of his senses – just as hunger amplifies a man's appetite so he appreciates his food far more. And this appreciation amounts to a sharper perception of the *difference* between roast beef and new potatoes and spring cabbage.

Our problem is to maintain this recognition of 'difference' even when our senses are tired. If we enter a room in total darkness, we do not assume that all the furniture has disappeared merely because we cannot see it. We *know* it is there. We need to impress this conviction of 'difference' upon our minds so deeply that we know it is there even when we cannot see it. What good would that do? It would prevent us from falling into the negativity that devastates our energy and sense of purpose – and which also happens to be the chief problem of all human beings. On a spring morning, when we can see endless 'difference' around us, and our minds are bubbling with optimism, it seems incredible that human beings can so forget this vision that they collapse into defeat, even into suicide. Yet Ouspensky himself clearly came close to suicide when he lost his Zinaida. So this question of difference is not merely an abstract philosophical issue; it is a matter of life and death.

It is this sense of urgency and excitement that makes *Tertium Organum* such a refreshing book. Ouspensky is on to something important – in fact, to *the* most important question, and he knows it. He senses that the experience on the Sea of Marmora, or walking towards the Peter and Paul fortress, could lead to a new way of living, a new kind of freedom. He is like a migratory bird that can smell its home. For more than 10,000 years, increasing knowledge has given man increasing power over his environment; but it has not, apparently, given him increasing power over himself. Yet Ouspensky has glimpsed the answer. Perception is like a spear thrown towards an object. But our innate pessimism and laziness prevent us from putting any force behind the throw. Our negativity means that we allow ourselves to 'leak' energy. Yet the mere recognition of what is wrong should enable us to put it right, to maintain an inner level of drive and optimism that would simply prevent us from being susceptible to such leaks.

Ouspensky asks:

First of all, what is the new knowledge?
    The new knowledge is *direct knowledge* by an inner sense. I feel my own pain directly; the new knowledge can give me the power to *sense*, as mine, the pain of another man.

What Ouspensky can feel, intuitively, is that if he can get rid of his tendency to negativity and self-doubt, his Russian melancholy, he can be a quite different kind of person. When we are asleep, or very tired, we lose even intuitive knowledge of ourselves; consciousness 'blurs'. When we are awake, we suddenly 'know' ourselves. If we were 10 times as awake – if our senses were far more highly energized – would we not 'know' other people with equal certainty? Our senses could be compared to flat batteries. How do we 'charge' them? By sheer 'concentrated attention', which has the same 'recharging' effect on the senses that driving a car has on the car battery. (Example: as you are reading this book, stop 'merely reading'. Concentrate your *full* attention; clench your fists, use the muscles of your face and forehead to focus your energies: *but go on reading*. Even a minute of this kind of effort will bring a curious sense of power and meaning, for your intellect is ceasing to work *in vacuo*, and is entering into active combination with your vital energies.) This is what the yogi strives for as he sits cross-legged, concentrating attention 'at the root of the eyebrows'. Unfortunately, Ouspensky's Western-style romanticism inclined him to discount this aspect of Eastern religion.

Tertium Organum ends with a chapter about mysticism, dealing with the phenomenon that R.M. Bucke called 'cosmic consciousness'. This, Ouspensky recognizes, is what the human race is evolving towards. He quotes the mystic Edward Carpenter:

> Men will not worry about death or a future, about the kingdom of heaven, about what may come with and after the cessation of life of the present body. Each soul will feel and know itself to be immortal, will feel and know that the entire universe with all its good and all its beauty is for it and belongs to it forever. The world peopled by men possessing cosmic consciousness will be as far removed from the world of today as this is from the world before the advent of self-consciousness.

This is a fundamentally Nietzschean view; it springs out of Zarathustra's recognition that the most basic answer lies in 'great health' – which, in turn, depends on *stopping ourselves from leaking*.

This is why Gurdjieff told Ouspensky that if he understood everything in his own book, he would be a great teacher.

Ouspensky's problem was that he had not yet grasped everything in his own book. He had, without knowing it, solved the basic problem of Ivan Osokin: the weakness, the self-pity, the Tchaikovskian melancholy. The basic solution lay in recognizing that they were analogous to the snail's perception of the sunlight, the darkness and the rain. Once the snail has learned that the limits of its shell are not the limits of the universe, it has also taken the most important step towards perceiving that universe as it really is, rather than as a stifling, trivial, petty, personal illusion.

These insights had thrown Ouspensky's mind into a ferment. He saw threads stretching out from his central idea to all kinds of apparently contradictory notions: Nietzsche's Superman, the message of the New Testament, yoga, the symbolism of the Tarot, dreams and hypnosis, the ideas of Einstein, Eternal Recurrence, mysticism, the importance of sex in the evolutionary scheme . . . The next task was to begin to get this explosion of insights and connections down on paper. And so, even before setting out for his trip to Egypt, India and Ceylon, he had started to write the book that would become *A New Model of the Universe*, a work that would contain the most important essay he ever wrote: the chapter called 'Experimental Mysticism'. He was still engaged upon this book when he met Gurdjieff.

Now we can begin to see why, in a certain sense, the meeting with Gurdjieff was Ouspensky's greatest personal disaster. He had already found his own answer, even if he did not know that he knew it. All he had to do was to pursue it, to think about it repeatedly until he had plumbed it to its depths. And at this point he met the man whose philosophy hurled him back into the pessimism of 10 years earlier. For Gurdjieff, man is a machine, a helpless puppet in the hands of fate. Eight years later, a young English doctor named Kenneth Walker would attend a talk by Ouspensky in a dreary room in Kensington, and would record Ouspensky's first words: that man likes to believe that he possesses a real and permanent 'I', whereas in fact he possesses dozens of 'I's', all struggling for possession; he is virtually a 'multiple personality'.

A man also prides himself on being self-conscious, whereas even a short course of self-study will reveal the fact that one is very rarely aware of oneself, and then only for a few fleeting moments. Man believes that he has will, that he can 'do', but this is also untrue. Everything happens in us in the same way that changes in the weather happen. Just as it rains, it snows, it clears up and is fine, so also, within us, it likes or it does not like, it is pleased or it is distressed. We are machines set in motion by external influences, by impressions reaching us from the outside world.

There is a simple objection to this: it is untrue. That is to say, it carries an accurate observation to a point at which it becomes untrue. The real trouble is that we allow our intellect and senses to operate *in vacuo*, and not in association with our vital forces, our sense of 'urgency'.

Now if Ouspensky had been as pessimistic as he sounds, he would not have been giving a lecture. His whole point – and Gurdjieff's – is that recognition of man's lack of freedom is the first step towards *achieving* some kind of freedom. Man must do this by struggle, by 'work on himself', by self-observation. The problem for Ouspensky's listeners, as Walker and a dozen others have made clear, is that his gloomy outlook communicated itself to his audience, producing the opposite effect to that he would have produced if he had spent the evening talking to them about the ideas of *Tertium Organum*. Walker notes that the room, with its uncomfortable chairs, reminded him of the Presbyterian churches of his Scottish childhood, and of the congregation awaiting the arrival of the minister – who would tell them they were all damned. This, in effect, is what Ouspensky was doing. This is what Gurdjieff did to Ouspensky.

The objection to Ouspensky's view can be stated simply. The basic problem for human beings is to break through to higher levels of energy, to what William James called – in an important essay – 'Vital Reserves'. James started from the recognition that there are certain days on which we feel more alive than on others. Much of the time, 'most of us feel as if a sort of cloud weighed upon us . . . *Compared to what we ought to be we are only half awake.*' James recognized that we are, at least, half awake, not fast asleep:

> In some persons this sense of being cut off from their rightful resources is extreme, and we then get the formidable neurasthenic and psychasthenic conditions, with life grown into one tissue of impossibilities, that so many medical books describe.
>
> Stating the thing broadly, the human individual thus lives usually far within his limits; he possesses powers of various sorts which he habitually fails to use. He energises below his *maximum*, and he behaves below his *optimum*. In elementary faculty, in coordination, in power of *inhibition* and control, in every conceivable way, his life is contracted like the field of vision of an hysteric subject – but with less excuse, for the poor hysteric is diseased, while in the rest of us, it is only an inveterate *habit* – the habit of inferiority to our full self – that is bad.

He goes on to ask how unusual men manage to escape these limitations, and answers – exactly as Gurdjieff answered:

> Either some unusual stimulus fills them with emotional excitement, or some unusual idea of necessity induces them to make an extra effort of will. *Excitements, ideas, and efforts*, in a word, are what carry them over the dam.

He goes on to make an observation that was also the basis of Gurdjieff's 'Work':

> In these 'hyperaesthetic' conditions which chronic invalidism so often brings in its train, the dam has changed its normal place. The slightest functional exercise gives a distress which the patient yields to and stops. In such cases of 'habit-neurosis'

a new range of power often comes in consequence of the 'bullying-treatment,' of efforts which the doctor obliges the patient, much against his will, to make. First comes the very extremity of distress, then follows unexpected relief.

Gurdjieff's basic method was to combat 'habit-neurosis' through a version of the 'bullying treatment' – by forcing his followers to make efforts that brought 'the very extremity of distress', followed by a sudden sense of freedom, as if a strait-jacket had been loosened.

William James had arrived at these conclusions through unpleasant personal experience. In *The Varieties of Religious Experience*, he describes how, at the age of 28, he fell into a state of general pessimism about his prospects:

I went one evening into a dressing-room in the twilight to procure some article that was there; when suddenly there fell upon me without any warning, just as if it came out of the darkness, a horrible fear of my own existence. Simultaneously there arose in my mind the image of an epileptic patient whom I had seen in the asylum, a black-haired youth with greenish skin, entirely idiotic, who used to sit all day on one of the benches, or rather shelves against the wall, with his knees drawn up under his chin, and the coarse grey undershirt, which was his only garment, drawn over them inclosing his entire figure. He sat there like a sort of sculptured Egyptian cat or Peruvian mummy, moving nothing but his black eyes and looking absolutely non-human. This image and my fear entered into a species of combination with each other. *That shape am I*, I felt, potentially. Nothing that I possess can defend me against that fate, if the hour should strike for me as it struck for him. There was such a horror of him, and such a perception of my own merely momentary discrepancy from him, that it was as if something hitherto solid within my breast gave way entirely, and I became a mass of quivering fear. After this the universe was changed for me altogether. I awoke morning after morning with a horrible dread at the pit of my stomach, and with a general sense of the insecurity of life that I never knew before, and that I have never felt since. It was like a revelation; and although the immediate feelings passed away, the experience has made me sympathetic with the morbid feelings of others ever since. It gradually faded, but for months I was unable to go into the dark alone.

In general I dreaded to be left alone. I remember wondering how other people could live, how I myself had ever lived, so unconscious of that pit of insecurity beneath the surface of life. My mother in particular, a very cheerful person, seemed to me a perfect paradox in her unconsciousness of danger, which you may well believe I was very careful not to disturb by revealing my own state of mind.

James's problem was that he had, like the neurasthenic patients, fallen into a state of gloom in which life had 'grown into one tissue of impossibilities', an endless series of hurdles that he lacked the strength to tackle. This sense of helplessness, of will-lessness, had sapped his 'vital reserves' until, so to speak, his inner-resistance gave way – plunging him into a state in which *nothing seemed worth the effort* – hence the sudden identification with the green-faced patient.

He describes how he succeeded in emerging very slowly from this slough of despond when he came upon a definition of free will by the French philosopher Charles Renouvier: 'the sustaining of a thought *because I choose to* when I might have other thoughts'. Renouvier had commented that we may feel that all our actions are mechanical, an automatic response to stimuli, until we consider the fact that *we can think one thing rather than another.* I can *decide* what to think; I can switch my train of thought from one track to another, and back at will to the first track. I can summon up images of rain, of snow, of July sunshine, of autumn gales, all merely by willing it.

The moment James saw that Renouvier was correct, he began to emerge from his hopeless gloom, and he struggled his way back to the state of intense creative activity in which he wrote his classic *Principles of Psychology.*

It is clear that this *intellectual conviction* that he possessed free will made all the difference between sickness and health. If he had continued to believe himself a machine, he would have continued to be undermined by misery and self-doubt. It follows that if James had met Gurdjieff at that fateful point in his life, and accepted his view that we possess virtually no free will, he might never have made a complete recovery from his neurasthenia.

So it becomes possible to see what went wrong for Ouspensky after his meeting with Gurdjieff. When he had finished *Tertium Organum* in 1911, he had an excited sense of being on the verge of discovering *the* answer. It was obviously very close, and something to do with maintaining a high level of excitement and 'eagerness'. His friend who could see 'difference' all the time was obviously near to it.

And at this crucial point, Gurdjieff explained to him that the first thing he must understand was that *he could do nothing*, plunging him back into something like William James's state of inner paralysis. Ouspensky must have known this was nonsense. By pursuing his goal in his own way, he had achieved a great deal. What he needed now was to maintain that high level of drive and optimism that had inspired *Tertium Organum*, and that was now inspiring *A New Model of the Universe*. But Gurdjieff was an impressive teacher. He seemed to know all the answers.

To begin with, there was self-remembering. This was an exercise that involved looking at an object, and making an effort to be aware of *yourself looking at it*. Anyone can see how difficult this is. Close your eyes and become aware of yourself. Now open them and look at your watch. Instantly, you cease to be aware of yourself and become aware of your watch. 'You' disappear. With a considerable effort, you can reawaken awareness of yourself as you look at your watch, but if you are not careful, you then 'forget' your watch and become aware only of yourself. (On the other hand, if you concentrate your attention while reading this book, you will note that you become aware of yourself as well as of the book.)

Ouspensky recognized that all moments of happiness are moments of self-remembering. What happened on the Sea of Marmora was a flash of self-remembering. What happened when he sensed the *difference* between the factory chimneys and the prison walls was self-remembering. We often experience self-remembering when setting out on a journey.

But if we think about this for a moment, we see the reason why. Because we feel relaxed, and we are *looking forward* to what is to come, we experience a feeling of *eager expectation*, the feeling that the world is a fascinating and delightful place. The same thing happens if we experience sudden relief when we had been expecting something unpleasant to happen – like a man being reprieved from a firing squad. The answer lies in that surge of optimism.

The American psychologist Abraham Maslow made the same discovery when he studied healthy people, and discovered that all healthy people had frequent 'peak experiences', experiences of sudden overwhelming happiness. Such people were good 'copers'; they tackled problems in an almost competitive spirit, enjoying the sensation of overcoming them. Maslow also discovered that when he talked to his students about peak experiences, they began recalling their own past peak experiences – many of which they had half forgotten – and they *began having peak experiences all the time*. Talking about peak experiences made them feel happy and optimistic, and this feeling was the major step towards having another peak experience. This is a matter to which we shall return in the final chapter.

Maslow's 'copers', then, were in a sense the opposite of the young and romantic Ouspensky, with his feeling that life is a trap. They were fundamentally 'realistic', and expected to solve problems with enough effort. The same 'realism' is also to be found – unexpectedly – in the young Albert Camus after he had escaped a 'death sentence' by tuberculosis. Although Camus had concluded that life is meaningless – he called it 'absurd' – he nevertheless found himself experiencing an 'intensity of physical joy' which even produced a kind of pleasure in 'the absurd'. In an essay in a volume called *Nuptials* (*Noces*) he described standing on the beach at Djemila, in Algeria, and experiencing a sense of living reality. Thinking about death, he reflects:

> I do not want to believe that death opens out on to another life. For me it is a closed door . . . All the [religious] solutions which are offered to me try to take away from man the weight of his own life. And, watching the heavy flight of the great birds in the sky at Djemila, it is exactly a certain weight in my life that I ask for and that I receive . . .

This is again a description of self-remembering, and Camus makes the important point that it involves a sense of 'the weight of his own life', like a burden that he is glad to shoulder, a sense of the real. Or it might be compared to a strong and healthy horse that enjoys pulling a cart, enjoys the feeling of the harness pressing into its chest and shoulders as it exerts its strength. Nietzsche said that happiness is the feeling that obstacles are being overcome, and this is again the secret of the peak experience.

Of equal interest in this context is the way that human beings lose their 'sense of the real'. We can see that when William James began to experience anxiety about his future, and a consequent feeling of depression, it was precisely this 'weight of his own life' that he had lost. The harness was hanging loosely around him, producing a sense of purposelessness. Nietzsche experienced the same thing in his teens, particularly after reading Schopenhauer and being convinced that life is 'absurd'. Simone de Beauvoir writes:

> I look at myself in a mirror, tell myself my own story, I can never grasp myself as an entire object. I experience in myself the emptiness that is myself, I feel that I am not.

Thinking too much and having too little purpose usually produces this sense of emptiness, particularly in the young.

Three

The Master

GEORGE IVANOVICH Gurdjieff was born on 28 December, 1877, so he was therefore less than a year older than Ouspensky.[1] He was born in Alexandropol, a Turkish town which had recently fallen to the Russians in the Russo–Turkish war. Gurdjieff's father was Greek, his mother Armenian. His father was a carpenter who was also a 'bard', able to recite thousands of verses from memory. When Gurdjieff saw in a magazine some verses from recently discovered tablets of the *Epic of Gilgamesh* – the world's earliest literature – he was impressed that they were exactly as his father recited them; the oral tradition had remained accurate over 4,000 years. This led Gurdjieff to the speculation that other kinds of ancient knowledge might have survived just as long, and inspired him to embark upon the same quest as Ouspensky.

Unlike Ouspensky, Gurdjieff spent his childhood surrounded by 'miracles'. He witnessed a paralytic crawl to the tomb of a saint and walk away cured. He was present when a drought ended suddenly as a procession carrying a miracle-working icon prayed for rain. He was present at a séance when a table rapped out answers to questions with one of its legs. A half-witted fortune-teller accurately foretold that he would have an accident with a firearm. He saw a Yezidi boy unable to break out of a circle that children had drawn around him, and in later years, it took Gurdjieff and an equally strong friend to drag a Yezidi woman out of such a circle. These were all mysteries to which Gurdjieff's highly active intelligence demanded an answer.

Gurdjieff had a highly developed practical inclination; he

could mend almost anything, and at one point made a living weaving carpets. But his earliest inclination was to become a priest. He was always deeply religious; the word 'God' came easily to his lips. (Ouspensky, on the other hand, discouraged his students from thinking or talking about religion.) In spite of this, he was cheerfully amoral where money was concerned. As a young man he helped to survey the proposed route of a railway, and approached the leading men in town or villages through which the railway was scheduled to pass, offering to 'fix' a station there – for a price.

As a teenager, Gurdjieff set out with a friend called Pogossian looking for the secrets of the 'Sarmoung Brotherhood' which supposedly dated from 2500 BC. He went to Smyrna, then to Egypt, Jerusalem and India. In the book in which he describes these adventures, *Meetings with Remarkable Men*, he claims to have spent three months in a monastery in the Himalayas, where – he hinted – he had discovered some of the 'secret knowledge' he was looking for.

At some point Gurdjieff learned about hypnosis from a teacher called Ekim Bey, and seems to have become a professional hypnotist, even hiring a hall in Tashkent to put on a 'magical' show. But he did not accept that hypnotism was merely 'suggestion'. He believed that it depends upon accumulating and concentrating a certain 'life force'. In later life, as we shall see, he often demonstrated this hypnotic or 'magical' ability.

Gurdjieff differed from Ouspensky in another basic respect: his attitude to sex was totally unromantic. He boasted to Bennett about the number of his illegitimate children, and spoke of women 'in terms that would have better suited a fanatical Muslim polygamist'. To begin with, Ouspensky seems to have been unaware of this aspect of Gurdjieff; when he found out, it seems to have been one of the factors that led to the break that lasted the rest of his life. (Gurdjieff's deliberately 'unreasonable' demands were another.)

In 1909, in Tashkent, Gurdjieff embarked on his career as a 'teacher', with a heavy emphasis on 'occultism'. Interest in Spiritualism, Theosophy and Rudolf Steiner's

Anthroposophy was intense, and Gurdjieff was soon regarded as a master of the occult – although he admits frankly that his reputation was largely the result of his 'skill in producing tricks'. He also became a highly successful businessman, running stores, restaurants and cinemas, and trading in cattle. By 1914, he was ready to realize his ambition of launching an 'institute' in Russia – he chose Russia because it was 'peaceful, rich and quiet'. The 1914 war was to bring these plans to nothing.

This, then, was the man Ouspensky met in March 1915: a hypnotist and 'magician', a Casanova (although he was now married to one of the Tsarina's ladies-in-waiting), something of a charlatan, yet basically a man who had acquired a profound knowledge of human nature.

There was one fundamental difference between Gurdjieff and Ouspensky. Gurdjieff, as we have seen, had learned some of the basic tricks of building up his vitality, and of using this vital power to gain influence over others. For example, everyone who met him commented on the penetration of his gaze. He was a man without self-doubt. Ouspensky was an intellectual and a romantic who had looked for his solutions in books: books about the fourth dimension, about Einstein, about yoga, about mysticism and cosmic consciousness, about the Kabbala and the Tarot and psychology. He felt that the question of freedom must be approached scientifically – that is, intellectually. He was fascinated by Gurdjieff because Gurdjieff seemed to be offering a comprehensive *system*, something his intellect could get its teeth into. Like all intellectuals, he was inclined to underestimate the importance of the body and the emotions.

In Moscow, Gurdjieff fascinated Ouspensky by the sheer range of his knowledge. When they talked about art, Gurdjieff explained that most of what we call art is mere fantasy and subjectivity. But, he said, there is such a thing as 'objective art', which is a kind of mathematics. There are objective works of art – like the Sphinx – which can be read like books, 'not only with the mind, but with the emotions, if they are sufficiently developed'. He went on to describe a statue which he had come across in Central Asia, in the desert at the foot of the Hindu Kush.

> At first it produced upon us simply the impression of being a curiosity. But after a while we began to feel that this figure contained many things, a big, complete and complex system of cosmology. And slowly, step by step, we began to decipher this system. It was in the body of the figure, in its legs, in its arms, in its head, in its eyes, in its ears, everywhere. In the whole statue there was nothing accidental, nothing without meaning. And gradually we understood the aim of the people who built this statue. We began to *feel* their thoughts, their feelings. Some of us thought that we saw their faces, heard their voices. At all events, we grasped the meaning of what they wanted to convey to us across thousands of years, and not only the meaning, but all the feelings and the emotions connected with it as well. That indeed was art!

As he travelled back to Petrograd from Moscow on the train, Ouspensky asked himself: is it possible that Gurdjieff actually *knew* what had to be known in order to proceed from words or ideas to deeds, to 'facts'? And although he could not answer the question positively, he 'had an inner conviction that something had already changed for me and that now everything would go differently'.

For readers of *Tertium Organum* and *A New Model of the Universe*, the absurdity is that – as Gurdjieff himself admitted – Ouspensky *already* 'knew' an enormous amount – perhaps almost as much as Gurdjieff could teach him. This is nowhere more apparent than in the chapter of *A New Model of the Universe* called 'Experimental Mysticism'.

Here, Ouspensky describes how, in 1910, he began a series of experiments whose aim was to explore 'mystical' consciousness. He does not explain how he went about it, but a reference to William James's *Varieties of Religious Experience* suggests that he simply used nitrous oxide, 'laughing gas', diluted heavily with air. James had already noted that nitrous oxide can produce a state when 'depth beyond depth of truth seemed revealed to the inhaler. This truth fades out, however, or escapes at the moment of coming to.'

Ouspensky also found himself frustrated by a similar problem:

> A change in the state of consciousness as a result of my experiments began to take place very soon, much more quickly and easily than I thought. But the chief difficulty was that the new state of consciousness which was obtained gave at once so much that was new and unexpected, and these new and unexpected experiences came upon me and flashed by so quickly, that I could not find words, could not find forms of speech, could not find concepts, which would enable me to remember what had occurred even for myself, still less to convey it to anyone else.

One of his central insights was that:

> All that we half-consciously construct with regard to the unknown is completely and utterly wrong. The unknown is unlike anything that we can suppose about it. The complete unexpectedness of everything that is met with in these experiences, from great to small, makes the description of them difficult. First of all, everything is unified, everything is linked together, everything is explained by something else and in its turn explains another thing. There is nothing separate, that is, nothing that can be named or described *separately*. In order to describe the first impressions, the first sensations, it is necessary to describe *all* at once. The new world with which one comes into contact has no sides, so that it is impossible to describe first one side and then the other. All of it is visible at every point; but how in fact to describe anything in these conditions – that question I could not answer.

William James had arrived at the same conclusions in an essay called 'A Suggestion About Mysticism': that states of mystical intuition may only be very sudden and very great extensions of the ordinary 'field of consciousness'. In other words, the mystic simply 'sees further', as if he has suddenly become a bird and can see into the distance. Naturally, he could not possibly describe all he sees at once; in fact, without a great deal of training, he would find it very difficult to describe anything at all, just as most of us would find it impossible to start putting into words the view from an aeroplane.

James went on to mention three 'mystical glimpses' that he had experienced, and goes on:

> In each of the three like cases, the experience broke in abruptly upon a perfectly commonplace situation and lasted perhaps less than two minutes. In one instance I was engaged in conversation, but I doubt whether the interlocutor noticed my abstraction. What happened each time was that I seemed all at once to be reminded of a past experience; and this reminiscence, ere I could conceive or name it distinctly, developed into something further that belonged with it, this in turn into something further still, and so on, until the process faded out, leaving me amazed at the sudden vision of increasing ranges of distant fact of which I would give no articulate account. The mode of consciousness was perceptual, not conceptual – the field expanding so fast that there seemed no time for conception or identification to get in its work. There was a strongly exciting sense that my knowledge of past (or present?) reality was enlarging pulse by pulse, but so rapidly that my intellectual processes could not keep up the pace. The *content* was thus entirely lost to retrospection – it sank into the limbo into which dreams vanish as we gradually awake. The feeling – I won't call it belief – that I had had a sudden *opening*, had seen through a window, as it were, distant realities that incomprehensibly belonged with my own life, was so strong that I cannot shake it off today.

This also makes us aware of Ouspensky's problem as a 'teacher' as well as a learner. The 'vision' expanded 'pulse by pulse' so that his intellect could not keep pace with it. So, clearly, Ouspensky's intellectual approach to the problem of a wider reality would never work; it would be like trying to cross the Atlantic in a rowing boat.

In these 'mystical' states, as on the Sea of Marmora, Ouspensky found that the relation between the 'objective' and the 'subjective' ceased to apply:

Here I saw that the objective and the subjective could change places. The one could become the other. It is very difficult to express this. The habitual mistrust of the subjective disappeared; every thought, every feeling, every image, was immediately objectified in real, substantial form which differed in no way from the forms of objective phenomena; and at the same time objective phenomena somehow disappeared, lost all reality, appeared entirely subjective, fictitious, invented, having no real existence.

Ouspensky compares this world to 'a world of *very complicated mathematical relations*':

. . . this means a world in which everything is connected, in which nothing exists separately and in which at the same time the relations between things have a real existence apart from the things themselves; or possibly, 'things' do not exist and only 'relations' exist.

Another writer on mystical experience, R.H. Ward, described (in *A Drug-Taker's Notes*) how, under dental gas,

I passed, after the first few inhalations . . . directly into *a state of consciousness already far more complete than the fullest degree of ordinary waking consciousness* [my italics], and that I then passed progressively upwards . . . into finer and finer degrees of this heightened awareness . . . This sense of upward movement continued until it seemed to me that I was rapidly passing through what I afterwards told myself was a 'region of ideas.'

This is clearly Ouspensky's region of mathematical relations.
To speak of relations as 'real' sounds paradoxical (after all, relations can change from moment to moment), but a little reflection can make the meaning clearer. In fact, we are so accustomed to things being 'connected' that we take it for granted. When I utter a sentence my 'meaning' is present in my head before I begin it, but I recognize that I can only express this meaning *in time*, by uttering words. I take the 'connectedness' of the words for granted – unless I am feeling

very tired, and I 'forget what I was going to say'. In such a moment we catch a glimpse of the consciousness of James's idiot, staring blankly at the world, 'seeing' everything yet unable to make the *connections* which would give it meaning. Meaning *is* 'connectedness', but not connectedness in time.

This, in turn, makes us aware that there is something very unsatisfactory and dull about our 'normal' perception. It 'sticks', like someone trying to plod over a very muddy field in heavy gumboots. We take this 'sticking' for granted until we are in moods of happiness and excitement, when we have the 'bird's eye view' in which we see things *related to one another*, and realize that our normal perception, in which they are separated from one another like the steps of the man in gumboots, like words in a sentence, is quite misleading.

To put it another way, what Ouspensky and James and Ward experienced was a brief glimpse of what 'normality' *should* be like ('far more complete than the fullest degree of ordinary consciousness') and that our present 'normality' is quite abnormal – or rather, sub-normal.

So, in effect, Ouspensky was in a state of intense *excitement*, in which consciousness seemed to be flowing faster. Normally, it is as slow and as solid as a glacier; in mystical states, the ice melts and it flows like a river.

This also becomes clear from Ouspensky's remark that he found it impossible to complete a sentence, because between every word, so many ideas occurred to him that he was unable to catch up. He began a sentence: 'I said yesterday . . .'

No sooner had I pronounced the word 'I' than a number of ideas began to turn in my head about the meaning of the word, in a philosophical, in a psychological and in every other sense. This was all so important, so new and profound, that when I pronounced the word 'said', I could not understand in the least what I meant by it. Tearing myself away with difficulty from the first cycle of thoughts about 'I', I passed to the idea 'said', and immediately found in it an infinite content. The idea of speech, the possibility of expressing thoughts in words, the past tense of the verb, each of these ideas produced an explosion of thoughts, conjectures, comparisons and associations. Thus, when I pronounced the word 'yesterday' I was already quite unable to understand why I had said it. But it in its turn immediately dragged me into the depths of the problems of time, of past, present and future, and before me such possibilities of approach to these problems began to open up that my breath was taken away.

Again, this is all quite logical. When consciousness is 'unfrozen' it ceases to be 'serial', like the words in a sentence, and becomes 'simultaneous' – that is, turns into a bird's eye view. It is obviously very similar to the state called 'inspiration', in which an author or musician has to write at top speed to keep up with his insights.

This image makes us aware that human beings are trapped in time, carried along by it as if on a river. Meanings flash past, like advertisement billboards on the bank, but it is hard to read them. Yet every time we become 'absorbed', every time we pay total attention to some meaning, we cause time to *slow down*. This is one of the most interesting things about the human condition: that we possess this power to 'slow time down'. It implies that, if we wanted to, we could somehow bring time to a halt and be in the presence of meaning. Ordinary men take it for granted that they are the slaves of time, and that, like an ever-rolling stream, it will carry them into oblivion. Philosophers and mystics glimpse this possibility that time is not an absolute; if we could learn to use our powers correctly, we could control it.

Ouspensky had practical experience of the 'non-absoluteness' of space and time. He describes how, after half an hour of intense discipline, 'I could quite clearly see the faces of people at a distance at which normally one would have difficulty in distinguishing one figure from another.' Space had 'telescoped'. On another occasion, he recalled his intention of making a trip to Moscow when he was in the midst of his 'experiments':

Suddenly, without any warning, I received the comment that I should not go to Moscow at Easter. Why? In answer to this

I saw how, starting from the day of the experiment . . . events began to develop in a definite order and sequence. Nothing new happened. But the causes, which I could see quite well and which were there on the day of my experiment, were evolving, and having come to the results which unavoidably followed from them, they formed just before Easter a whole series of difficulties which in the end prevented me from going to Moscow. The fact in itself . . . had a merely curious character, but the interesting side of it was that I saw what looked like a possibility of calculating the future – the whole future was contained in the present. I saw all that had happened before Easter resulted directly from what had already existed two months earlier.

Ouspensky's insight is a direct contradiction of modern 'Chaos Theory', which asserts that, because of the basic mathematical laws of 'chaos', no physical process (the weather, for example) is predictable for more than a day or two ahead.

In mystical states, the normal *sense* of time, which is 'serial', also vanishes – or rather, Ouspensky says, 'Together with it or within it there appeared as it were another feeling of time, and two moments or ordinary time, like two words of my sentence, could be separated by long periods of another time.' In other words, moments of 'serial time' were separated by flashes of 'bird's eye time', extending 'crosswise' like another dimension.

We can begin to see why mystics find it so difficult to express what they see. It is not that mystical consciousness is contradictory or illogical. It is simply that 'ordinary consciousness' is based on a set of false suppositions about the absoluteness of time, and that the initial problem is to explain why something that seems 'common sense' and self-evident is full of misconceptions and errors. At one point in his experiments, Ouspensky tried hard to summarize his new insights so he could recall them later, and wrote a sentence on a sheet of paper. When he read what he had written the next day, it was: 'Think in other categories.' In other words, these insights involved a totally different *approach* to what we call reality, a recognition that most of our *premises* are wrong.

Another long passage that describes this sense of immense richness and multiplicity has even wider implications. Ouspensky describes sitting on a settee and looking at a copper ash-tray. Again, it aroused 'a whirlwind of thoughts and images' – where did copper come from, how had it been discovered, how had people learned to work it, how is a modern ash-tray made . . . ? He tried to express this 'whirlwind' of thoughts on paper, and read the next day: *'One could go mad from one ashtray.'*

But what fascinated him in retrospect was the feeling that 'the ash-tray was alive', 'that it thought, understood and told me all about itself'. 'Everything is alive,' I said to myself . . . 'there is nothing dead, it is only we who are dead.'

(Another Gurdjieff disciple, C. Daly King, had experienced a similar vision on a New Jersey railway platform: the bricks of the station 'appeared to be tremendously alive . . . seething almost joyously inside and [giving] the distinct impression that . . . they were living and actively liking it'. People, on the other hand, 'looked dead, really dead'.[2])

This led Ouspensky to the recognition that:

> Everything was living, everything was conscious of itself. Everything spoke to me and could speak to everything. Particularly interesting were the houses and other buildings that I passed, especially the old houses. They were living things, full of thoughts, feelings, moods and memories. The people who lived in them were their *thoughts, feelings, moods.*

(It is interesting to note that Ouspensky later achieved this same sense of the 'personality' of houses from doing Gurdjieff's self-remembering exercises. It should also be clear that Gurdjieff was describing the same sensation when he spoke of the statue at the foot of the Hindu Kush, and gradually began to understand the thoughts and feelings of those who made it until he felt that the statue was able to 'speak' to him.)

Ouspensky goes on:

I remember once being struck by an ordinary cab-horse in the Nevsky, by its head, its face. It expressed the whole being of the horse. Looking at the horse's face I understood all that could be understood about a horse. All the traits of horse nature, all of which a horse is capable, all of which it is incapable, all that it can do, all that it cannot do; all this was expressed in the lines and features of the horse's face. A dog once gave me a similar sensation. At the same time the horse and the dog were not simply horse and dog; they were 'atoms', conscious, living 'atoms' of great beings – 'the great horse' and 'the great dog.' I understood then that we are also atoms of a 'great being', 'the great man.' A glass is an atom of a 'great glass.' A fork is an atom of a 'great fork'.

In other words, Ouspensky was seeing Plato's world of ideas as a reality, a point also made by R.H. Ward: '. . . it seems to me very interesting that one should thus, in a dentist's chair and the twentieth century, receive practical confirmation of the theories of Plato.' All this was experienced in 'an exceedingly intense emotional state':

My attitude towards this new knowledge was in no way indifferent; I either loved it or was horrified by it, strove towards it or was amazed by it; and it was these very emotions, with a thousand others, which gave me the possibility of understanding the nature of the new world I came to know.

It is important to note that Ouspensky felt that his method of obtaining these insights – through laughing gas – was the wrong way. He says that he felt that there was *somebody* who watched me all the time and often tried to persuade me to stop my experiments, not to attempt to go along this path, which was wrong and unlawful from the point of view of certain principles which I at that time felt and understood only dimly'. The basic principle is, in fact, self-evident. There is no point whatever in having thousands of insights if you cannot hang on to them in some way.

J.G. Bennett was to describe a similar experience in the forest at Fontainebleau in 1923, when a tremendous bout of 'super-effort' raised him into the 'exceedingly intense emotional state' in which he was able to evoke feelings at will: [3]

> . . . I said to myself: 'I will be astonished.' Instantly I was overwhelmed with amazement . . . Then the thought of fear came to me. At once I was shaking with terror. Unnamed horrors menaced me on every side. I thought of 'joy', and I felt my heart would burst from rapture. The word 'love' came to me, and I was pervaded with such fine shades of tenderness and compassion that I saw that I had not the remotest idea of the depth and the range of love. Love was everywhere and in everything. It was infinitely adaptable to every shade of need. *After a time, it became too much for me, it seemed that if I plunged any more deeply into the mysteries of love, I would cease to exist.* [My italics.] I wanted to be free from this power to feel whatever I chose, and at once it left me.

Bennett goes on to quote Blake's lines:

> Grown old in love, from seven to seven times seven
> I oft have wished for hell for change from heaven,

and adds:

> I realised that for Blake this was no mere trick of words, but the expression of a real experience. I knew that the world I had entered was one where there is no loneliness, because all who enter into that Eternal Source meet there as brothers.

Bennett's vision of the infinite varieties of love leaves no doubt that he had entered the same state of 'unfrozen' consciousness as Ouspensky – with a sense of the infinite 'connectedness' of everything – and that he had soon had enough of it. What is the good of being *shown* the answer if it promptly escapes us, due to our inability to capture it in words and concepts? Our *job*, as Ouspensky well knew, is to capture 'visions' in words and concepts, so they become permanently available to all men. The main business of writers is to trap 'meanings' in words – as if someone had invented a camera to take

photographs of the advertisement signs as they flash past us –
so that other men can examine them at leisure. The main
point of this exercise is to fill us with courage and certainty,
so we no longer have any doubt about our purpose and
direction.

Now in fact, it had precisely the opposite effect on
Ouspensky:

> The experiments almost always ended in sleep. During this
> sleep I passed into the usual state and awoke in the ordinary
> world, in the world in which we awake every morning. But this
> world contained something extraordinarily oppressive, it was
> incredibly empty, colourless and lifeless. It was as though
> everything in it was wooden, as if it was an enormous wooden
> machine with creaking wooden wheels, wooden thoughts,
> wooden moods, wooden sensations; everything was terribly
> slow, scarcely moved, or moved with a melancholy wooden
> creaking. Everything was dead, soulless, feelingless.
>
> They were terrible, these moments of awakening in an unreal
> world after a real one, in a dead world after a living, in a limited
> world, cut into small pieces, after an infinite and entire world.

But it was Ouspensky's innate romanticism that made this
attitude inevitable. He could see no advantage in 'frozen' (or
as he calls it, 'wooden') consciousness. This is again why
Ouspensky felt that it was somehow wrong for him to
experiment with nitrous oxide. He was not yet ready for a
glimpse of an 'infinite and entire world', and it only filled him
with a longing for a 'land of lost content'. He failed to realize
that a world 'cut into small pieces' is far more easily *recorded*
than an 'infinite and entire world'. So he was unable to *grasp*
the meaning of his extraordinary glimpse of the answer to all
his questions.

Yet on one level at least, that meaning should have been
clear. A 'bird's eye view' raises us above the materiality of
everyday life, and enables us to see it from a distance. This
is what happens when we study history or philosophy or
become absorbed in a work of art. They also enable us to
contemplate our world with a new sense of 'connectedness'.

And it is the *intellect* that enables us to take this 'bird's eye view'. In a sense, therefore, the author of *Tertium Organum* and *A New Model of the Universe* was already on the right path before he met Gurdjieff, and his later distrust of the 'way of intellect', of 'mere ideas', was unjustified.

This is something that becomes very clear as we read the rest of *A New Model of the Universe*. The chapter on Experimental Mysticism is followed by a chapter called 'In Search of the Miraculous',[4] in which we can sense that Ouspensky was gradually coming closer to his 'answer'. It is a series of descriptions of various places: Notre Dame, the Pyramids, the Sphinx, the Buddha with sapphire eyes in a temple near Colombo, the Taj Mahal, all of which Ouspensky regards as forms of 'objective art' that can speak directly to human beings. Gurdjieff might have dismissed these descriptions as mere 'poetry'. But because Ouspensky *is* a poet, they convey more than his intellectual speculations. He felt that the Buddha with the sapphire eyes was communicating to him:

> All the gloom that rose from the depths of my soul seemed to clear up. It was as if the Buddha's face communicated its calm to me. Everything that up to now had troubled me and appeared so serious and important, now became small, insignificant, unworthy of notice . . .

Ouspensky was beginning to recognize that his problem was that he had never outgrown the pessimistic romanticism that pervades *Ivan Osokin*.

Unfortunately, there is a sense in which his chance to outgrow it ended when he met Gurdjieff. Ouspensky's interpretation of Gurdjieff's teaching was that man possesses very little freedom – so little that even *highly directed* efforts seldom achieve their purpose. 'Man can do nothing: he is a machine controlled by external influences, not by his own will, which is an illusion,' Ouspensky told Bennett a few years later.

There is one basic objection to this, an objection that might

be regarded as the central point of this book: *if it was true, then
how is it that Ouspensky was able to achieve so much before he met
Gurdjieff?*

Clearly, what Ouspensky needed when he returned to
Russia in 1914 was to follow his own creative path, to try to
pursue the implications of his vision on the Sea of Marmora,
to try to grasp the significance of the 'difference' he had
sensed as he looked at the Peter and Paul fortress; above all,
to understand of the 'connectivity' of his nitrous oxide visions.
A New Model of the Universe is still full of that spirit of eagerness
and enthusiasm that infuses *Tertium Organum*. This applies
particularly to the remarkable chapter on the superman. It is
full of statements that seem a flat contradiction of his view that
will is an illusion:

> We have indeed no grounds whatever for denying the
> possibility of a real, living superman in the past, or in the
> present, or in the future. At the same time, we must recognise
> in our inner world the presence of seeds of something higher
> than that by which we ordinarily live, and we must recognise
> the possibility of the sprouting of these seeds and their
> manifestation in forms at present incomprehensible to us.

A few paragraphs later, he expresses an insight that came from
his mystical experiences:

> An intellectual approach to the idea of superman is possible
> only after a very long and persistent training of the mind.
> Ability to think is the first necessary stage of the initiation . . .
> What does it mean to be able to think? It means to be able to
> think differently from the way in which we are accustomed to
> think, that is to say, to conceive the world in new categories.
> We have simplified our conception of the world too much, we
> have become accustomed to picture it to ourselves as too
> uniform, and we must learn anew to understand its
> complexity.

All this is practically a contradiction of his 'Gurdjieffian
approach'. 'We have simplified our conception of the world too

much.' Why? Because we see it *robotically* or mechanically, so we have as little idea of reality as a snail has of the sun, the darkness and the rain. We must learn to 'think in different categories', to grasp the *difference* between things which our 'mechanicalness' irons out. Ouspensky is not telling us that free will is an illusion, that we have so many 'I's' that thinking is virtually a waste of time – an attitude that already plants the seeds of doubt that undermines the 'peak experience', the mood of eager expectancy, which is the starting point of achievement. He is telling us that, behind the rather gloomy façade of everyday reality, there are endless reasons for optimism.

This becomes even clearer in the final chapter of *A New Model of the Universe*, entitled 'Sex and Evolution'. Here Ouspensky distinguishes between what he calls 'infra-sex', the low form of sexual consciousness in which sex is both 'dirty' and comic, and what he calls 'normal' sex, which is altogether closer to D.H. Lawrence's vision of sex as a transformative force. What Ouspensky has recognized is that sexual desire, a man's response to a woman and vice versa, is one of the best examples of the consciousness of 'difference', and that this difference is real, not illusory. A man who sees something of the 'eternal feminine' in a woman is seeing her more truly than a man who merely sees her as an instrument of his own pleasure, or a biological organism for continuing the species. Finally there is 'supra-sex', in which we sense that sex is a glimpse of a new consciousness, a higher reality:

> Mystical sensations undoubtedly and incontestably have a taste of sex . . . Of all we know in life, only in love is there a taste of the mystical, a taste of ecstasy. Nothing else in our life brings us so near to the limit of human possibilities, beyond which begins the unknown.

Here again, we have that sense of 'new worlds' which makes *Tertium Organum* so exciting.

All this must be qualified by admitting that it would be inaccurate to say that Ouspensky entirely lost this sense of poetry and excitement when he came under the influence of Gurdjieff. In fact, to begin with, he obviously found Gurdjieff's ideas the most exciting he had so far encountered. Yet as we study his exposition of these ideas in *In Search of the Miraculous*, we can also begin to see how the original excitement turned into something much more down to earth, 'scientific', and how this scientific approach slowly gave way to the pessimism of his comment that 'there is only one hope – that we should find the way to find the way to work with the higher emotional centre. And we do not know how this is to be done.'

Yet when we turn from *A New Model of the Universe* to Ouspensky's account of his meeting with Gurdjieff in *In Search of the Miraculous*, it is possible to understand that original excitement. At one of their earliest meetings, Ouspensky asked Gurdjieff about his ballet *The Struggle of the Magicians*. This is, in fact, a pleasant little love story about a wealthy man who tries to seduce the pupil of a white magician by enlisting the help of a black magician; the white magician foils his plans, but the rich man finally becomes his disciple, and the ballet ends with the suggestion that love will triumph in the end. Gurdjieff explained that the most important part of the ballet was its dances, then went on to compare them to the movements of an orrery – a device simulating the movements of the planets. In the same way, he explained, in 'sacred dances', the movements are intended to remind those who understand them of certain hidden laws of nature. Such mysterious hints were guaranteed to fascinate Ouspensky. It was the same when Gurdjieff began to talk about what he called 'the ray of creation' – the sun, the planets and the moon – and to explain that they are living beings, and that the moon is a planet in the process of birth, which may evolve to the same level as the earth. Gurdjieff was later to explain that the universe has seven levels of reality, and that the moon is the lowest of these; those who live on that level are subject to 96 laws. Man, who lives on the earth level, is subject to 48 laws. And so on up the 'ray of creation: the planets, the sun, the galaxy, the totality of worlds, the absolute, each being subject to half as many laws as the previous level, until we reach the absolute, which is subject only to its own law . . .' All this seemed to Ouspensky to reveal that Gurdjieff was the repository of the kind of secret knowledge that he had spent his life searching for.

Even so, much of what Gurdjieff had to say only reinforced Ouspensky's romantic pessimism. For example, when they sat in a noisy café speaking about the war (Gurdjieff deliberately chose such places to force Ouspensky to make 'extra effort'), Gurdjieff explained that war was the result of planetary influences. When two planets approached too closely to one another, the result was a kind of tension, such as the tension one might feel when passing too close to someone on a narrow pavement. Ouspensky asked: 'Then is there absolutely nothing that can be done?', and Gurdjieff replied gloomily: 'Absolutely nothing.'

Not all Gurdjieff's pronouncements were quite so negative. He explained, for example, that man is in prison, and that it is possible to dig a tunnel to freedom – but that one man alone can do nothing. The tunnel can only be completed by a group working together:

> Furthermore, no one can escape from prison without the help of those *who have escaped before*. Only they can say in what way escape is possible, or can send tools, files or whatever may be necessary. But *one* prisoner alone cannot find these people or get into touch with them. An organisation is necessary. Nothing can be achieved without an organisation.

For a loner like Ouspensky, such a notion was a violation of his deepest instinct: the feeling that a man can find his own salvation, but not that of others. At the very end of his life he was to return to this belief.

On another occasion, Gurdjieff told his pupils the grim little parable of the magician and the sheep. A magician gets tired of the wanderings of his sheep, who were aware that they were due to be slaughtered and skinned. So he hypnotizes them and tells them that they are immortal and no harm can come to them. He also tells them that he is a good master who loves his flock. Finally, he suggests that they are not sheep at all; some he convinces that they are lions, others eagles, others men, others even magicians . . . And so the sheep stayed quietly at home until it was time for them to be slaughtered . . . This, explained Gurdjieff, 'is a very good illustration of man's position.'

As he absorbed such notions, Ouspensky must have felt that all the insights and glimpses of *Tertium Organum* and *A New Model of the Universe* were illusory, and it says a great deal for his stubborn self-belief that he still went on to complete and publish *A New Model of the Universe*.

The real problem, of course, was that Gurdjieff and Ouspensky were completely different types. Ouspensky was the intellectual romantic; Gurdjieff was the man of action. There is a sense in which Ouspensky was totally unsuited to putting Gurdjieff's method into practice. Gurdjieff's fundamental insight was the same as William James's: that it is 'some unusual idea of necessity' that induces people to make the extra efforts of will that 'carry them over the dam'. Most of us are aware that we actually need physical experience to relax and expand consciousness – experience such as travel, exercise, love-making, socializing, even eating and drinking. So Gurdjieff never lost sight of the importance of physical effort. He treated all his disciples as 'neurasthenics' who needed the 'bullying treatment', or as people suffering from snakebite who need to be forced to walk up and down to keep them awake.

Ouspensky, however, was simply not the type to appreciate the 'bullying treatment'. He had already glimpsed the mystical world of total 'connectivity', William James's 'distant horizons of fact'. His most powerful desire was to establish contact with the higher centres, so he could continue to make forays into these unknown realms, and learn more of their geography. Gurdjieff was able to teach him many interesting techniques – involving complex physical movements, strenuous exercise, and breathing exercises – but these failed to achieve the results Ouspensky hoped for. Yet in abandoning his own work in favour of Gurdjieff's, he had also turned his back upon his own peculiar genius.

1. J.G. Bennett obtained this date from Gurdjieff's passport. Other sources give his date of birth as 1873, a date I have accepted in other accounts of Gurdjieff (for example, in *The Occult*).
2. Daly King's mystical experiences are cited more fully in the penultimate chapter of my *Beyond the Occult*.
3. A fuller version of this story – from Bennett's autobiography *Witness* (Chapter 10) – is quoted in the opening chapter of my book on Gurdjieff in this series.
4. This is also the title given by his editors to Ouspensky's last book, describing his years with Gurdjieff, to which Ouspensky himself gave the title 'Fragments of an Unknown Teaching'.

Four

Creating 'Man Number Four'

STILL, IT would be grossly unfair to Gurdjieff to imply that Ouspensky was fascinated solely by his hints about hidden knowledge and 'sacred mysteries'. Ouspensky was 'hooked' because he was an intellectual, and Gurdjieff's ideas formed a powerful and consistent intellectual system. Let us, before we go any further, look more closely at this system.

Human beings, says Gurdjieff, 'grow up' to a certain point, and then stop. Up to that point they are 'subsidized' by nature. But further growth can only be brought about by immense personal effort. When one of Gurdjieff's later pupils was asked to define the aim of 'the Work', she replied: 'To prevent your past from becoming your future.'

This notion is obviously common to all religious disciplines, whose aim is 'spiritual growth'. So is the notion of strenuous effort to obtain this growth – saints flogging themselves with whips, yogis sleeping on beds of nails or sitting cross-legged in the same position for weeks at a time. Where Gurdjieff differs is in his far more pragmatic approach. In order to obtain a certain result, he says, it is necessary to know precisely what you want to obtain. Saints and ascetics have so far recognized three ways: the way of the fakir, the way of the monk, and the way of the yogi. The way of the fakir is the way of physical control, the attempt to dominate the body by will-power. The way of the monk is the way of faith and religious emotion; by attempting to dominate feelings. The way of the yogi is the way of the mind; aiming to gain total control of the mind. But there is a 'Fourth Way', which Gurdjieff calls the way of the 'sly man', but which might equally well be translated as 'intelligent man'. This is the attempt to approach the problem of personal evolution through intelligent understanding, and it combines all three previous ways. Ouspensky's experiments with nitrous oxide might be regarded as an example of the Fourth Way: he was trying to take a short cut to a certain kind of knowledge, and his attempt was partially successful.

Closely connected with this notion of the four ways is Gurdjieff's assertion of the four aspects of man, which he compared to a carriage, a horse, a driver and the owner of the carriage. The carriage is the physical body, the horse is the feelings and desires, the driver is the mind, and the owner is the 'higher self' – the part that Gurdjieff was trying to bring into being through the Work. The energies used by these four are in an ascending ladder of refinement, the physical being the coarsest and the 'owner's' the highest. Our task is to *transmute* these various energies into higher levels.

But the heart of Gurdjieff's 'System' lies in his distinction between 'essence' and 'personality'. Personality is the part of us that we develop to enable us to cope with the world – a kind of defence system. The underlying reality, the inner self – the part the Work is designed to develop – is our essence. Typically, Gurdjieff explained that one of the few men of essence he had met was a Corsican brigand, who had developed it by spending days in the hot sun, peering down the sights of his rifle, waiting for travellers to rob.

Personality encloses us like a shell. We like to believe that inside that shell is our 'true self', the 'real me'. In fact, says Gurdjieff, we are full of thousands of little 'I's. They could be compared to the crystalline fragments that a windscreen shatters into when struck with a hammer. But every time we make some tremendous effort, two of the crystals fuse together. If we could make enough efforts, we would finally obtain one solid block of crystal. If that could happen, man would be virtually a god.

Our aim, then, is to make the kind of effort that will create enough 'friction' to fuse two crystals together. These efforts Gurdjieff calls 'intentional suffering'. This does not mean flogging ourselves or seeking out misery, but simply making efforts of will instead of drifting along in a robotic or mechanical state.

Self-remembering is a form of 'intentional suffering'. It should be noted that self-remembering does not necessarily entail the strenuous effort of looking at your watch and trying to be aware of yourself looking at it. It merely means maintaining alertness. At the end of *The Struggle of the Magicians*, the white magician prays: 'Lord Creator, and all you, His Assistants, help us to be able to remember ourselves at all times in order that we may avoid involuntary actions, as only through them can evil manifest itself.' This clearly means vigilance and alertness. Thomas de Hartmann tells how self-remembering once saved his life. Gurdjieff's words 'Remember yourself' meant very little to him. But when he was acting as a dispatch rider, and a shell blew him off his horse, he refused to panic, but kept repeating: 'I remember myself.' Keeping his head, he caught his horse and rode off, while shells continued to fall around him. It can be seen that, in this case, self-remembering simply meant maintaining self control. (As an interesting footnote to all this, we may observe that when we succeed in maintaining states of self-remembering, one odd consequence is often the occurrence of what Jung called 'synchronicities', absurd 'coincidences' that seem to be somehow designed to show us that we are on the right track.)

According to Gurdjieff, our central problem is that we are so 'mechanical' that we slip into robotic states without even noticing. Emergencies or crises wake us up. If we could devise some form of 'alarm clock', this would solve the problem – which is undoubtedly why some people seem to cause themselves problems and crises. Gurdjieff's solution was to form groups; then the members could co-operate in keeping one another awake. In general, Gurdjieff's Work consisted in a series of disciplines designed to keep his pupils in a high state of self-awareness.

There is another aspect of the teaching that explains the deep impression it made on the pupils: Gurdjieff's 'cosmology'. We have already touched upon this in speaking of Gurdjieff's teaching on the 'planets' and the 'ray of creation'. Everything in the universe is subject to two laws: the Law of Three and the Law of Seven. We are inclined to think in terms of two forces: positive and negative, darkness and light. Gurdjieff insisted that there is always a third, a neutralizing or reconciling force (he later spoke of Holy Affirming, Holy Denying, and Holy Reconciling). In the Work, the first force is man's desire to change, the second is his laziness and inertia, the third is the new knowledge that can bring about the change. Even the Absolute is composed of three forces, which is why the next level down from it, called the totality of all worlds, is subject to three laws. If human beings live passively, making no attempt to create 'essence', when they die they collapse to the very lowest level – the moon – and become 'food for the moon', subject to 96 laws and almost incapable of freedom.

The Law of Seven concerns the energies of the vibrations of the universe, and is obviously connected with the seven levels of the 'ray of creation' (moon, earth, planet, sun, solar system, totality of worlds and Absolute – these, of course, should not be regarded literally as *the* moon, *the* earth, and so on, but as levels of being). Gurdjieff explained that the basic vibrations of the universe can be understood by studying the seven musical notes of the tonic scale. There are, he said, two 'weak points' in the scale, between mi and fa, and between ti and doh, and these are the two points where, in actuality, vibrations slow down. These breaks in the scale mean that when we set out to do something, we quite unconsciously change direction at these two points – without even noticing it – and may even end by doing the opposite of what we set out to do. The solution is to apply 'reinforcements' at these two points, and so keep the energies moving in a straight line, so to speak. So, according to Gurdjieff, all attempts to transform oneself will be wasted without some knowledge of the Law of Seven.

Gurdjieff also laid enormous emphasis on a figure he called the Enneagram: a circle with a triangle in it and each side of the triangle subdivided into two more points. The

Enneagram, he said, was a symbol of his whole cosmology, showing the basic laws of the universe. The nine vertices symbolize the seven notes of the octave and the two 'breaks' (although in the Enneagram the break between ti and doh does not seem to be in the right place).

If man is to progress smoothly up the octave of evolution, he needs 'shocks' to help him over the breaks. It is the teacher's job, said Gurdjieff, to administer such shocks, and this obviously explains why he gave his pupils such a hard time.

We can now at least begin to see why Gurdjieff's teaching left his pupils in such a state of excitement. It all seemed to make practical sense, yet it offered a method of 'salvation' that gave it a religious dimension. This is why Ouspensky, like the rest, felt that he had finally received the 'revelation' he had been searching for all his life. Gurdjieff's System provided a practical method of pursuing the aims that he had always explored in a vague and uncoordinated manner. It offered a way of turning his life into a continuous effort to pursue the insights of his nitrous oxide experiences – a way that he could now feel was entirely 'lawful'.

But with the benefit of hindsight, we can see certain things that were not apparent to Ouspensky. The most important of these is that Gurdjieff deliberately *exaggerated* problems to galvanize his pupils into maximum effort. So, for example, when Ouspensky asked about life after death, Gurdjieff replied that most people are so mechanical that there is nothing in them that can survive death. Only when a man has created some degree of 'essence' is there something that can 'survive'. The 'astral body' is not something everybody possesses; it has to be created by strenuous effort and 'friction'. Yet at another time, Gurdjieff told Ouspensky that objects belonging to a dead person contain 'traces' of that person, which enable those still living to maintain contact. And Bennett tells the strange story of how, after he had lost his mother, Gurdjieff had remarked: 'She is in need of help because she cannot find her way by herself. My own mother is already free and can help her.' He then taught Bennett strenuous visualization exercises that finally – after agonizing effort – succeeded in 'summoning' the presences of Gurdjieff's mother and his own. Both stories seem to indicate an unqualified acceptance of life after death.

There was also exaggeration in Gurdjieff's assertion that most people are machines who possess no freedom whatever. The title of the third volume of his 'testament', *All and Everything,* is *Life is Real Only Then, When 'I Am'*, and it is clear that we all experience the feeling that 'life is real' in all moments of happiness and excitement. In other words, we all experience the 'I am' feeling a thousand times. It does *not* require strenuous effort. Gurdjieff is again exaggerating to keep his pupils 'up to the mark'.

Let us try to reformulate Gurdjieff's basic insights without the exaggeration.

Human beings *are* largely machines. The heart is a pump, the brain is a computer, the joints are levers. And we have achieved our supremacy as the leading species on earth because of the sheer complexity of our mechanism. We all possess a 'robot' who does things for us. When I learn something new – to drive a car, to speak a foreign language – I have to do it painfully and consciously, step by step; then my 'robot' takes over and does it for me. The human robot has learned to handle a complexity of experience that would drive any other animal to nervous breakdown.

Our problem is that such complexity tends to be self-defeating – like owning a library so huge that even the catalogue is a library in itself.

One might say that human beings are 50 per cent 'robot' and 50 per cent 'real person'. When we are happy and excited, the proportion changes: we become 49 per cent 'robot' and 51 per cent 'real'. These are the moods of 'holiday consciousness' in which we feel happy and wide awake – the moods of 'I am'. In our ordinary daily activities we are roughly 50/50. But as soon as we become tired, we become 51 per cent 'robot' and 49 per cent 'real person'.

Human beings could be compared to motor cars whose batteries recharge as they drive. If a car is left standing in a garage for months, its batteries get flat. Humans have an additional problem: when they do things 'mechanically', they also fail to recharge their vital batteries. It is only when we are driven by a sense of purpose and optimism that we recharge our batteries. Abraham Maslow described a case of a female patient who was so bored with her job in a factory that she became completely devitalized, even ceasing to menstruate. When Maslow learned that she had hoped to make a career in sociology, but had been forced to take the factory job to support her family, he advised her to study sociology at night school. As soon as she did this, the symptoms disappeared. Her sense of purpose was now recharging her batteries. The 'peak experience' could be regarded as a kind of spontaneous discharge of a highly charged battery, a spark of sheer joy.

Now in recognizing that our main problem is that we are too 'robotic', Gurdjieff could see that the basic necessity is to instil into people a high level of purpose. The robot causes us to go 'slack', so that our response to life becomes sluggish and dull. At best we experience the 50/50 state. At worst, we spend most of our time in a 51 per cent robot-state. And this tends to cause boredom and discouragement, so that problems plunge us into depression – which could be regarded as 52 per cent robot. The more robotic we become, the harder it is to escape, for our low vitality prevents us from making the effort required. Such states are extremely dangerous, for we can fall into a condition of permanent *passivity*, merely 'reacting' to life. In these states we become deeply vulnerable, physically as well as emotionally. A California psychiatrist, Wilson van Dusen, has described how long-term mental patients can become totally passive, staring at a television set all day, and continuing to stare even when it is turned off. This is an excellent image of what is wrong with human consciousness. And long-term passivity can produce physical as well as mental illness.

This explains why Gurdjieff felt justified in 'exaggerating'. And if a person can be galvanized into a sense of urgency, surely that is all that matters?

But we have seen that one problem of exaggerating man's

mechanicalness is that it tends to produce a grim and negative state of mind. Gurdjieff told Ouspensky: 'One need not . . . be afraid of efforts; the danger of dying from them is not all that great. It is much easier to die from inaction, from laziness, and from the fear of making efforts.' But, as we shall see, Gurdjieff's critics have accused him of being a bully who drove some of his followers into illness, and even – in one well-known case, the writer Katherine Mansfield – into death.

A year after meeting Gurdjieff, Ouspensky began to feel that he was at last beginning to understand the Work. On first meeting the Moscow pupils, he felt that they were artificial, as if playing a role; by the summer of 1916 he saw that this was because they were maintaining a high level of self-observation. Gurdjieff, he noticed, also observed them closely, and placed them in new situations where they would cease to behave formally – for example, taking them on excursions into the countryside or a trip up the Neva. Later on, in Paris, he would organize large dinner parties for the same reason, and force everyone to drink toast after toast in vodka until they were all drunk. He explained to Ouspensky: 'Later on you will see that everyone in the Work is given his own individual tasks corresponding to his type, and his chief feature or his chief fault, that is, something that will give him the opportunity of struggling more intensively against his chief faults.'

The task he gave Ouspensky was to act as a kind of propagandist, to lead his acquaintances into conversations about the Work. When the whole group was instructed to talk to their acquaintances about the Work, the results made them aware of how difficult it is to communicate meaningfully, even with intelligent people. (Ouspensky was later to go to the opposite extreme and order his followers not to discuss the Work with anyone outside it.)

At other meetings, Gurdjieff tried the experiment of asking his pupils to talk about themselves and their lives. This was also a failure; it turned into an exercise in anecdote that bored everybody. But Ouspensky realized something interesting:

that when he began to speak, there were many things that he had no intention of divulging.

On another occasion, Ouspensky was in a gloomy mood and complained to Gurdjieff that he felt they were getting nowhere. To cheer him up, Gurdjieff offered to answer any question. Ouspensky asked about the truth of 'Eternal Recurrence', and Gurdjieff replied – perhaps predictably – that Eternal Recurrence *is* a reality, but that work on oneself can nevertheless alter a man's possibilities. This was a view that Ouspensky incorporated into a revised version of *Ivan Osokin* (the early version had ended on a totally pessimistic note).

Ouspensky was galvanized to new efforts. He began short but intensive fasts without worrying about their effect on his health, as well as practising breathing and concentration exercises. Gurdjieff invited a small group of his pupils to a house in Finland – not far from Petrograd – and was unusually harsh and sarcastic, as if trying to provoke them. He certainly upset Ouspensky when he repeated in front of everyone something unflattering about one of their number which Ouspensky had told him in the greatest confidence.

Here we encounter the essence of the problem that finally caused the break between the two men. Ouspensky was, of course, fully aware that Gurdjieff was attempting to galvanize them into effort, like an experienced drill sergeant, and that a man who wishes to become a good soldier does not quarrel with the drill sergeant. Yet he must also have been aware that he possessed his own genius, and that he already knew a great deal even before he met Gurdjieff. So he felt that Gurdjieff was going too far in repeating a confidence. *Was* he correct? The question is of fundamental importance. Was Gurdjieff underestimating Ouspensky's 'freedom'? If so, then Gurdjieff himself was capable of misjudgement, even of a kind of stupidity. Ouspensky himself later decided that the answer to that question was yes. Those who regard Ouspensky as a man of genius in his own right will agree.

Almost as if to apologize for his 'bullying' treatment, Gurdjieff now allowed Ouspensky an experience of his 'magical' powers. One evening in Finland, Gurdjieff called three of his pupils into a room, and proceeded to show them certain postures and physical exercises. Gurdjieff always laid great emphasis on physical movements as training for man's 'moving centre'. Anyone who wishes to try out their effect should make an attempt to pat himself on the head with one hand while rubbing his stomach with the other. Gurdjieff's 'movements' often involved doing something different with both hands, both feet, and the head. On this occasion, Ouspensky was impressed by the precision of Gurdjieff's movements. After this, Gurdjieff began to discuss why they could not tell the story of their lives:

> And with this the miracle began.
> I can say with complete assurance that Gurdjieff did not use any kind of external methods, that is, he gave me no narcotics nor did he hypnotise me by any of the known methods.
> It all started with my beginning to *hear his thoughts* . . . Suddenly I noticed that among the words which he was saying to us all there were 'thoughts' which were intended for me. I caught one of these thoughts and replied to it, by speaking aloud in the ordinary way. Gurdjieff nodded at me and stopped speaking. There was a fairly long pause. He sat still saying nothing. After a while I heard his voice inside me as it were in my chest, near the heart. He put a definite question to me . . . I answered him in the affirmative . . . And he at once put another still more definite question to me in the same way . . . And again I answered in the same way. Z and S [Zaharoff and Stoerneval] were visibly astonished . . . This conversation . . . proceeded in this fashion for not less than half an hour.

Back with the others, Gurdjieff made some remark about Ouspensky that drove Ouspensky to walk out in the woods. Suddenly, he saw that Gurdjieff was right:

> . . . what I had considered to be firm and reliable inside myself . . . did not exist. But I had found something else. I knew that he would not believe me and that he would laugh at me if I showed him this other thing. But for myself it was indubitable, and what happened later showed that I was right.

This is an interesting passage because it reveals something that Ouspensky prefers not say openly: that Gurdjieff taunted him about his weakness and his romanticism. This is something that Ouspensky takes care not to reveal in all his work; yet it remains, as Gurdjieff would have said, his 'chief feature'.

We can also see that, if Ouspensky was right in feeling that he had discovered another source of strength within himself, the implication must be that Gurdjieff himself was *not* infallible; his psychological insight was limited, and there were things about Ouspensky that he discounted and failed to understand.

Back in his own room, Gurdjieff again began to speak 'inside [Ouspensky's] chest', and they held a conversation while Gurdjieff was out on the veranda with others. Ouspensky is again reticent, but it is clear that Gurdjieff was trying to force him to make some promise, or to leave the Work. He gave Ouspensky a month to make up his mind.

The next morning, at breakfast, Gurdjieff again read Ouspensky's mind, and advised him to stop thinking about a certain question. During the next few days, Ouspensky found himself in a strange emotional state, so that he remarked to Gurdjieff: 'How can this be got rid of? I cannot bear it any more.' Gurdjieff's reply was that this was what Ouspensky had been asking for. He was now awake. Ouspensky comments that he is not certain that this was entirely true.

Back in Petrograd, Ouspensky not only continued to converse with Gurdjieff – who was on the train going to Moscow – but to actually see him.

At this time, he says, he also began seeing 'sleeping people'. As he walked along the street, he would see that people were actually asleep, surrounded by their dreams in the form of clouds. When this impression began to fade, he found he could renew it by efforts of self-remembering.

All this convinced Ouspensky that 'paranormal' powers are a by-product of higher states of awareness, and that therefore they cannot be studied 'objectively', as if in a laboratory. The mind needs to be 'awake' first.

In fact, as we have seen, Ouspensky had already made the same discovery during his nitrous oxide experiments. He had 'heard voices' which were sometimes able to reply accurately to his questions, and had also correctly foreseen the precise events that would cause the trip to Moscow to be cancelled.

Ouspensky adds that this higher state of awareness also made him see, with great clarity, why violence is always bound to be counter-productive. This recognition, he says, was not 'ethical', but practical.

Soon after this, Gurdjieff announced to the group that they all had to make a choice: now they must decide whether they wanted to wake up, or remain asleep. 'In future I shall work only with those who can be useful to me in attaining my aim.' Two people dropped out of the group. It seems clear that what Gurdjieff was demanding of Ouspensky in Finland was total commitment – perhaps to devote his life to spreading the idea of the Work. Ouspensky seems to have agreed.

It may have been Gurdjieff's recognition of what was happening in Russia that caused him to make these demands. The war was going badly; troops were fighting without weapons and without proper clothing. In an offensive that ran out of steam, the Russians lost a million men. The army was demoralized. Many people believed the Tsarina – who was of German birth – wanted the Germans to win. At the end of 1916, the Tsar's *eminence grise* Rasputin was assassinated by Prince Felix Yussupov; he had foretold that if he was killed by a member of the aristocracy, the Russian monarchy would come to an end. In March 1917, riots and strikes broke out in Petrograd, and there was a general mutiny of troops. The Tsar abdicated, and a provisional government took control, while the royal family was placed under arrest. In April, Lenin arrived from Switzerland, sent by the Germans to undermine Russia. In July, the Bolsheviks made their first attempt to seize power.

In February, Gurdjieff had made his last visit to Petrograd; when he took his leave of his followers at the station, Ouspensky felt that something unusual had taken place. On the platform, Gurdjieff had seemed 'an ordinary man, like anyone else'. Moments later, when he came to the window of the train, he seemed quite different, 'a man of a quite different order . . . with a quite exceptional importance and dignity in every look and movement, as though he had suddenly become a ruling prince or statesman of some unknown kingdom . . .'

It is possible of course, that Gurdjieff was 'acting' again; most people who knew him felt that he wore a series of masks. But it seems more probable that Ouspensky and the others had witnessed a genuine transformation. This is what Gurdjieff had meant when he said, 'In future I shall only work with those who can be useful in attaining my aim.' He did not state his aim, but it can have been only one thing: he was using his group, and the consciousness induced by teaching them, to raise himself into a higher state of intensity. Ouspensky later observed that teaching other people had the effect of teaching himself. It seems probable that what they witnessed at Petrograd station was the moment in which Gurdjieff achieved his 'transformation' to a more conscious level of power. A journalist who travelled in the same carriage as Gurdjieff was convinced that he was, at the very least, a millionaire oil magnate.

And now, before we accompany Gurdjieff and Ouspensky on the flight that will take them into exile, it is time to pause to look back over what had happened since their meeting two years earlier.

It seems clear that when Gurdjieff left Tashkent and embarked on his career as a teacher in Moscow and St Petersburg, his teaching was still in an undeveloped form. He had almost certainly learnt his 'cosmology' – the 'ray of creation' – from monks or holy men in Central Asia or the Himalayas, and may have arrived at his conclusion that man is 'asleep' from painful personal experience. In the essay 'Glimpses of Truth', which Ouspensky had heard read aloud when he first met Gurdjieff's Moscow pupils, the emphasis is all on the Law of Three and on Gurdjieff's cosmology.

There seems no doubt that Gurdjieff deliberately set out to

'catch' Ouspensky. He admitted that when Ouspensky left on his trip to India and Ceylon, he instructed his pupils to carefully read his articles to determine what sort of man he was. The detailed care with which he answered questions in their early talks reveals how far he was determined to interest Ouspensky – who was by then a well-known lecturer and author. Gurdjieff wanted to become known, and the best way was to interest men who were already known – Thomas de Hartmann, who was already famous as a ballet composer, was another example.

But for most of the two years after he met Ouspensky, Gurdjieff simply talked. He also planned to present his ballet *The Struggle of the Magicians*, which was full of 'sacred dances'. But he had not yet developed the 'exercises' and methods that became the basic part of the Work after he left Russia. Ouspensky describes how they were introduced to the famous 'Stop!' exercise at Essentuki in 1917: Gurdjieff would shout 'Stop!', and everyone had to freeze, no matter what he was doing. (One man got his fingers severely blistered on a glass of boiling tea.) Gurdjieff explained that this exercise was considered sacred in 'schools', but it seems equally likely that he had just invented it. If not, why had he not mentioned it during the past seven years, since his teaching career began?

There can also be no doubt that his aim, in part at least, was to become a famous teacher. With new pupils, he insisted on total secrecy – they were not allowed to discuss the Work with anyone who was not part of it. Yet when Ouspensky declined to make such a promise, Gurdjieff gave way. And in later years, when Ouspensky had written down his early experiences with Gurdjieff in 'Fragments of an Unknown Teaching',[1] Gurdjieff read it and approved. He was not a charlatan, a man who wanted fame for its own sake. But he certainly did want fame. So it is important to realize that, although Gurdjieff struck his disciples as a superbeing, he developed, like anyone else, by a slow learning process.

The next three years were to see this learning process accelerated. As the Revolution began, Gurdjieff recognized

that it would no longer be possible to work in Russia. He sent
Ouspensky a postcard saying that he was going back home,
to Alexandropol. Ouspensky and the Petrograd group had
already decided to leave, so when Gurdjieff invited
Ouspensky to join him, he took a train for the Caucasus. In
Tiflis (now Tbilisi), the capital of Georgia, drunken soldiers
held meetings on the platform all night, and three were shot –
one for theft, the second because he was mistaken for the first,
and the third because he was mistaken for the second. In
Alexandropol, Ouspensky met Gurdjieff's family, and saw a
photograph of Gurdjieff that revealed 'with undoubted
accuracy what his profession had been at the time it was
made' – he adds that, since this was his own discovery, he will
keep it to himself. The photograph was the one that showed
Gurdjieff as a stage hypnotist. Ouspensky seems to have tried
to keep this aspect of Gurdjieff a secret, possibly because he
believed Gurdjieff used it for sexual purposes. (Gurdjieff was
later to reveal his former profession in his book *Herald of
Coming Good*, published in 1933.)

Ouspensky was impressed by Gurdjieff's filial respect for
his father and mother – the father was over 80. Gurdjieff
listened to his father's conversation for hours on end,
stimulating him with questions.

After two weeks they decided to return to Petrograd. But at
Tiflis they met a general who had been one of Gurdjieff's
pupils and what he told Gurdjieff made the latter change his
mind about returning. He left Ouspensky to go on alone. But
before that happened, an interesting conversation took place.
When Ouspensky asked how he could strengthen his 'I',
Gurdjieff told him that he should already be feeling his 'I'
differently. Ouspensky had to admit that he felt exactly the
same as usual. But two years later he was to experience this
sense of a 'controlling ego', the 'owner' of the horse and
carriage, and to know that his years with Gurdjieff *had* borne
fruit after all. 'Man number four' had come into being.

In Moscow and Petrograd, Ouspensky passed on to
Gurdjieff's students the message that they should join him in
the Caucasus. When he returned, Gurdjieff had moved to

Essentuki – not far away – and finally a group of 12 foregathered there. It included Ouspensky's wife and step-daughter, Thomas de Hartmann and his wife Olga, and a pupil called Zaharoff.

Here, during the next six weeks, Gurdjieff introduced them to the 'Stop!' exercise, and to the idea of 'super-effort' – deliberately pushing yourself further when tired. It seems to have been at this point in his career that Gurdjieff began to introduce the strenuous physical exercises that became such a central part of his method. A typical one is described by Ouspensky: sitting on the floor with knees bent and palms close together between the feet, the pupil had to lift one leg and count up to ten, saying 'Om' instead of using numbers, then up to nine, then up to eight, and so on, down to one, then start repeating it all backwards, meanwhile 'sensing' his right eye. Then he had to separate the thumb and 'sense' his left ear. And so on. When this exercise was mastered, the pupils had to add breathing exercises to it, and after that, still more 'complications' were introduced. In addition to this, they were all made to fast. And in spite of physical weakness, they were made to run for miles in the heat, stand with extended arms, or mark time at the double. All these, Gurdjieff explained, were merely 'preliminary' exercises.

But it was during these exercises that Ouspensky had his one experience of 'higher consciousness'. In a room alone, he began to mark time at the double while performing breathing exercises. As he was pouring with sweat and his head was spinning, 'suddenly something seemed to crack or move inside me and my breathing went on evenly and properly at the rate I wanted it to.'

I shut my eyes and continued to mark time, breathing easily and freely, and feeling exactly as though strength was increasing in me and that I was getting lighter and stronger. I thought that if I could continue to run in this way for a certain time I should get still more interesting results because waves of a joyful trembling had already begun to go through my body which, as I knew from previous experiments, preceded what

I called the opening of the inner consciousness. But at this moment someone came into the room and I stopped.

Ouspensky says that this taught him that an exercise can be transferred from the mind to the 'moving centre'. This clearly has much in common with William James's 'second wind' and with Bennett's experience at Fontainebleau (see p.55), when the 'breakthrough' was again achieved by strenuous and agonizing physical effort.

All at once, just as the pupils were beginning to feel that they were at last achieving something significant, Gurdjieff shocked them all by announcing that he was dropping the Work, and going to Tuapse, on the Black Sea coast. Ouspensky says that this was the moment when his faith in Gurdjieff first began to waver. It all seemed so pointless. He went to Tuapse with Gurdjieff, then decided to return Petrograd. He stayed there until after the Bolshevik takeover, then, feeling that 'something sickly and clammy was drawing near', he left for the Caucasus again. Ouspensky was to hate Communism with a total and virulent hatred all his life.

Meanwhile, Gurdjieff had decided to move a few miles down the coast, near to Sochi. Typically, he decided to make this a test for his followers. In his book *Our Life with Mr Gurdjieff*, Hartmann describes how Gurdjieff bought a cart, and told them they were going to take a short cut to Sochi over the mountains. The Hartmanns were sent on ahead, and found the climb exhausting in the heat, with their city clothing (Olga was wearing high-heeled shoes). They stopped at an inn for tea, hoping to stay the night, but when Gurdjieff arrived, he decided that the night was so fine that they might as well continue. They stumbled on exhaustedly until two in the morning, when Gurdjieff announced they would make a fire. It was raining, and they had to struggle through the undergrowth to find dry wood. Finally they made tea and most of them lay down to sleep on the hard stones. But Hartmann was told that he had to keep guard. He sat there until dawn, when Gurdjieff announced it was time to set off. Now Hartmann was told he could lie on top of the luggage.

In fact this was worse than walking, for if he dozed off, he fell off the luggage.

Finally, at midday, they passed through a village, bought cooked lamb and beans, and Hartmann had a deep sleep. That night, again, they needed a fire because they could hear the howling of wolves and jackals, which might have killed the horses. They took turns on guard. The next day at noon they found a deserted posthouse, and spent two days recovering. When they resumed their journey, Hartmann observed that he was no longer tired. The 'super-effort' had caused a breakthrough to a higher energy level, James's 'vital reserves.' Eventually, when they arrived at a pleasant little villa near Sochi, Hartmann felt he was in heaven. Nevertheless, he fell ill with typhoid and almost died; he attributed his recovery to the fact that Gurdjieff sat by his bed and somehow 'infused' vitality.

Ouspensky joined them there. So did a Petrograd disciple, Leonid Stoerneval. His wife had been deeply unwilling to leave Petrograd, but shortly after they left, the Bolsheviks took over. Hartmann had had a similar escape: the day after he left Petrograd, soldiers had come to his home to arrest him.

Again, Gurdjieff revealed the unpredictable part of his nature. For some reason, he turned against Zaharoff and virtually forced him to leave. Ouspensky was upset; his faith in Gurdjieff the man – as distinguished from the System – was beginning to collapse.

In February 1918, they moved to another village. The danger now was being cut off by the Bolsheviks. Then Gurdjieff decided to go back to Essentuki. Work there became harder still. They were ordered to fast and the men were separated from the women. The 'movements' became more and more complicated and difficult. The aristocratic Hartmann was made to go to Kislovodsk to sell silk wound on to cards – until Gurdjieff relented. The women were ordered to give up their jewellery, and Olga de Hartmann cried all night, but dutifully handed it over. Gurdjieff then gave it back to her. But another woman who handed over her jewellery, confident that she would receive it back, never saw it again. Gurdjieff seemed to be teaching in harshly practical parables.

While in Essentuki, Gurdjieff's family arrived – nearly 30 of them. Turks had invaded Alexandropol, and his father had been killed. Gurdjieff was forced to look after this crowd of starving relatives. It was as if fate was subjecting him to the same 'testing' that he was inflicting on his pupils.

Meanwhile, Ouspensky was now at last certain that he had to break with Gurdjieff:

> I saw clearly that I had been mistaken about many things that I had ascribed to G, and that by staying with him now I should not be going in the same direction I went at the beginning.

To try to explain his meaning, he says that if Gurdjieff had all the time been leading him into the 'way of the monk', he would have left – not because he did not respect the way of the monk, but because *it was not his way*. And neither, he felt, was the way the Work was now developing.

Ouspensky had at last recognized what, perhaps, he should have realized three years earlier. Yet he had undoubtedly received a great deal from Gurdjieff. In any case, there was now no going back. All he could do was to move to another house and continue work on *A New Model of the Universe*, as if the meeting with Gurdjieff had never happened.

1. Published as *In Search of the Miraculous*.

Five

Success

GURDJIEFF AND his followers left Essentuki at the beginning of August 1918, and made their way 100 miles southwest to the Black Sea. Gurdjieff had succeeded in escaping with his usual incredible effrontery. He had asked the Essentuki Soviet for permission to mount an archaeological expedition to the mountains where, he said, he hoped to find gold. He would need large quantities of alcohol for washing the gold. The Soviet provided the alcohol, together with the necessary tents and other equipment.

Ouspensky, who had also meant to go south, was trapped when Cossacks cut the railway line. So he was forced to spend the autumn and winter in Essentuki. He managed to get a job as a porter, then as a schoolteacher, and so was able to support a numerous 'family' – his wife, stepdaughter, and his stepdaughter's two children. He also started a school library with books that had been 'requisitioned' from their owners. When the White army re-took the town he had hurriedly to tear off the word 'Soviet' from the notice outside the Essentuki Public Library.

At the first opportunity, he finally made his way south, to Ekaterinodar (later Krasnodar), an evil-smelling and ugly city that he loathed on sight. There he began to write a series of articles about his experiences of the Revolution, which he sent off to London. They appeared in *The New Age*, the magazine edited by the charismatic Orage, whose acquaintance Ouspensky had made on his way to India in 1912, and renewed on his way back to Russia in 1914. Ouspensky's condemnation of the Bolsheviks was uncompromising; he talked of the 'dictatorship of the criminal element'.

When Ouspensky mentioned, in one of the letters, that he was 'only alive because my boots and my trousers and other articles of clothing . . . are still holding together', Orage hastened to contact F.S. Pinder, the British government representative in Ekaterinodar, who appointed Ouspensky to his staff, and seems to have paid him from his own pocket.

It was also while in Ekaterinodar that Ouspensky finally 'set up on his own'. He formed a small group and began to lecture to them on Gurdjieff's ideas. It was at this point that he suddenly became aware that now, at last, he was aware of a 'new I'. 'Man number four' was beginning to form inside him, and he experienced a curious new confidence. And in fact, in a sense – although there were still difficulties to come – his troubles were basically over.

But the Reds were winning the civil war. Denikin, the White general, was forced to withdraw to Rostov-on-Don, and the British staff – and the Ouspensky family – went with him. In Rostov Ouspensky met once again Andrei Zaharoff, the man Gurdjieff had driven away from Essentuki. Zaharoff had become totally disillusioned, not only with Gurdjieff, but also with his ideas, and Ouspensky found it impossible to convince him that, no matter what they might both think of Gurdjieff as a person, the ideas were still valid. Carl Bechhofer Roberts, a journalist connected with *The New Age*, spent two weeks with Ouspensky and Zaharoff in their lodging – a draughty barn – drinking home-made vodka. (His experiences are amusingly recorded in an appendix to Ouspensky's 1919 *Letters from Russia*.) A month later, Roberts had escaped to Novorossisk, on the Black Sea, Ouspensky was back in Ekaterinodar, and Zaharoff had died of smallpox. Finally, with the aid of the British, Ouspensky and his family were evacuated to a refugee camp on Prinkipo Island, a suburb of Constantinople. There, once again, he encountered Gurdjieff.

Gurdjieff's band of disciples was now greatly reduced. From Essentuki they had travelled to Maikop, escaped from there by the skin of their teeth as the Reds closed in, and returned

to Sochi. There, to everyone's astonishment, Gurdjieff
announced that the group would now break up. The likeliest
reason is that they had run out of money. A small number
remained, including Gurdjieff's wife, the de Hartmanns and
the Stoernevals. When the Turks withdrew from Georgia –
which they had been occupying – in late 1918, Gurdjieff
decided to return to its capital Tiflis. He arrived there in
January 1919, and found it an unexpectedly pleasant place to
resume his Work. It was full of artists and intellectuals who
had fled from the Bolsheviks, and was virtually a second
St Petersburg. Olga de Hartmann became a singer at the
opera; her husband became a professor at the Conservatoire.
Gurdjieff resumed his teaching, and acquired himself two
new disciples, the painter Alexander de Salzmann and his
wife Jeanne, a teacher of Jacques Dalcroze's system of dancing,
called 'eurythmics'. Gurdjieff attended some of Jeanne de
Salzmann's classes, and demonstrated some of his own
'movements'. But he was undoubtedly as much influenced by
eurythmics as was that other contemporary guru Rudolf
Steiner. Gurdjieff also organized a profitable carpet business.
It was in Tiflis that he decided to call his future institute the
Institute for the Harmonious Development of Man; he even
drafted a prospectus, declaring (untruthfully) that it was
already in operation in Bombay, Alexandria, Kabul, New York,
Chicago, Stockholm, Moscow and Essentuki. Ouspensky,
who received a copy, was not impressed. And Bechhofer
Roberts, who called at the new institute, reported that
Gurdjieff was getting tired of his followers and was anxious
to get to Europe. The newly independent Georgia was chaotic,
and likely to be attacked by the Reds (as, in fact, it was in 1921).
This is why, in May 1920, Gurdjieff and a group of about 30
followers started to make their way to Constantinople; they
arrived in June. They were all penniless – the carpets
Gurdjieff had tried to take with him as working capital had
been seized en route by marauding soldiers – and were forced
to start looking for ways of making money in a city that was
already crowded with poverty-stricken Russians.

Gurdjieff arrived to find that Ouspensky had already

started his own group. When his ex-Master arrived, the ever-loyal Ouspensky handed it over to him. Although he had decided not to work with Gurdjieff again, the two remained on friendly terms. Ouspensky then set up on his own at the White Russian Club in Pera, the European quarter, and his talents as a lecturer soon brought him such large audiences that he had to apply to an English lady for the loan of her drawing-room. Her name was Winifred Beaumont, and her flat was shared by a young English Intelligence officer called John Godolphin Bennett. Bennett had been invalided out of the army after being blown up – he had had an 'out of the body experience' in the hospital – and had gone one better than Ouspensky in concluding that the answer to the riddles of the world lay in the concept of a *fifth* dimension.

Bennett and Mrs Beaumont were intrigued to hear the noisy shouts that came from her drawing-room – they might have suspected a political meeting, but Ouspensky had given his word that politics would not be discussed, and they both felt he could be trusted. When Bennett asked Ouspensky what they were talking about, and Ouspensky replied, 'The transformation of man', Bennett was even more intrigued. In due course, and under separate auspices, he met Gurdjieff – whose name he already knew, since he had received notification from Indian Intelligence that Gurdjieff was a Russian agent.

Inevitably, he was entranced. When he and Mrs Beaumont were invited to watch the 'dances', they were deeply impressed by the 'Stop!' exercise – the more so as the dancers were all rushing towards them at top speed when Gurdjieff shouted the order. But for some reason, Bennett made no attempt to become part of the group.

Meanwhile, fate was arranging a pleasant surprise for Ouspensky. A young Russian named Nicholas Bessarabov had escaped from Russia after the Revolution, taking with him a copy of *Tertium Organum*, which had deeply impressed him. In America, he approached the well-known architect Claude Bragdon, who was the author of a book on the fourth dimension, and who spoke Russian. Bragdon was equally excited by *Tertium Organum*, and he and Bessarabov embarked on a translation. In 1920, Bragdon published the book himself (under the imprint Manas Press), and to his delight and astonishment, it sold 7,000 copies in its first year. He obtained Ouspensky's address from *The New Age*, and sent him some copies of the book, together with a cheque. It was probably the happiest day of Ouspensky's life. He lost no time in writing to Bragdon to ask him if he could help him to get to London or New York. Again, fate was working overtime on Ouspensky's behalf. As Bragdon was about to reply in the negative, he received a telegram from Lady Rothermere, the wife of the British newspaper magnate, saying that she was deeply impressed by *Tertium Organum* and would like to meet its publisher. The result of the meeting was a cable for £100 to Ouspensky, and an invitation to come to London with all expenses paid.

Fortune was smiling on Ouspensky. Probably only one person in Constantinople would have been able to obtain him a visa, and that person happened to be head of British Intelligence there – John Bennett. It took three months, but by August, the Ouspenskys were ready to sail.

They arrived to a fairy-tale reception. The beautiful Lady Rothermere, a blue-eyed blonde, threw a magnificent party for them, at which they ate with gold knives and forks from what looked like gold plates. The fairy-tale continued; when Ouspensky gave his first lectures in Lady Rothermere's studio in St John's Wood, they were attended by the cream of London's intelligentsia, including Orage, T.S. Eliot, Aldous Huxley, Gerald Heard, and a long list of doctors, psychologists, editors and other professional men. The British are notoriously impervious to ideas, but Ouspensky's build-up had been impressive: a mysterious foreign philosopher who had been forced to flee from the Bolsheviks, had endured immense hardships, and then, against all the odds, had made his way to London to present his new message. It all made him an irresistible attraction. And when the lectures turned out to be, in fact, startlingly new and strange, the conquest was complete. Ouspensky became the intellectual flavour of the month.

In retrospect, it is easy to understand why. The First World War had left behind a general feeling of nausea and disillusionment. Ezra Pound had written in *Mauberley*:

> There died a myriad,
> And of the best among them,
> For an old bitch gone in the teeth,
> For a botched civilisation.

It was the poem that, more than any other, inspired Eliot's *Waste Land*. This was the age of *The Waste Land*, of *Ulysses*, of Gertrude Stein's lost generation, of Hemingway's *The Sun Also Rises* and Scott Fitzgerald's tales of the jazz age. Orage himself had been virtually discovered by Shaw, who had financed *The New Age*. But Shaw was now regarded as outdated. Orage considered himself rather as a disciple of Nietzsche – a 'revaluer of values'. Even before the war, he had announced himself an 'immoralist', one who rejected all the old values. In this he was probably inspired more by the immensely successful novel *Sanine* by Artsybashev, in which the hero is the totally 'natural man', who believes that all the old sexual and religious values are illusions, like the emperor's clothes. Pre-war London had been obsessed by everything Russian, from the works of Tolstoy and Dostoevsky to the Diaghilev ballet, and novels like Andreyev's *Red Laugh* and Artsybashev's *Breaking Point* (in which virtually everyone commits suicide) had brought the notion of total moral negation to London long before *The Waste Land*.

A young man named C.S. Nott, who was to become one of Gurdjieff's most faithful followers, expressed the general malaise when he wrote:

> Although I had had a religious upbringing and . . . been a Sunday-school teacher and lay preacher . . ., organised religion now had no content for me, nor could it give me a satisfying answer to the questions that arose in me as a consequence of the disillusionment resulting from the war.

Disillusionment had become the watchword:

> Unreal city
> Under the brown fog of a winter dawn . . .

In this atmosphere of emptiness and boredom, everything seemed to be disintegrating. In music, tonality was dissolving into the discords of Schönberg and Stravinsky. In art, surrealism and Dadaism seemed to make a mockery of the tradition of centuries. In philosophy, the logical positivists announced that all talk of metaphysics and values was meaningless. In psychology, Freud's sexual theory reduced the unconscious mind to a basement full of decaying rubbish and religion to a communal lie.

And now, into this scene of desolation, came a prophet from Holy Russia, announcing devastating truths that also seemed startlingly original. Here was a complex system of ideas that satisfied the sceptical intellectuals, but which also asserted that salvation could be achieved by effort. None of his audience had ever heard anything remotely like it before. The most up-to-date of them were interested in Freud, Jung and Adler, but this new doctrine seemed to sweep everything before it like an autumn gale. After that first meeting, the stunned Orage told Claude Bragdon that 'Mr Ouspensky is the first teacher I have ever met who has impressed me with the ever-increasing certainty that he knows and can do.'

Yet the first impression Ouspensky made on his audiences was far from impressive. One hostile commentator, John Carswell, has written: 'Ouspensky, though strikingly large and blond almost to the point of albinism, was in some ways unimpressive.' The writer David Garnett thought he looked rather like Woodrow Wilson: 'The same lavish display of false teeth, the same baffled, unseeing eye, the same aura of high thinking and patent medicines.' Another member of his audience, Paul Selver, found Ouspensky 'quite monumentally boorish. He was one of those exasperating Russians who doggedly refuse to credit any other Slav nation with artistic ability. He sneered when I expressed the view that there were several Czech or Serbian poets of outstanding greatness. I had read them and he had not, but he contemptuously dismissed my remark with a sweeping gesture, as though consigning these unspeakable rhymesters to a garbage heap.'

Roland Kenney, a socialist who became editor of the *Daily Herald*, wrote, 'When sitting in reflection or repose, he hunched himself together and looked like a dejected bird huddling up in a rainstorm.' But he put his finger on the essential when he added: 'He was obviously a man of a dominant if not domineering type of character, with determination – or obstinacy – written over his every feature.' And another writer, Rom Landau, who also became an Ouspensky disciple, speaks of his 'strongly dictatorial manner'.

Ouspensky probably did not have the slightest interest in contradicting Selver's opinion of Czech and Serbian poets, and certainly no interest in exalting Russians at their expense; he was simply not interested in what he considered to be literary small-talk, or in questions he regarded as a waste of time. When one lady in his audience asked if the Buddha had reached the seventh level of consciousness, he replied, 'I don't know' without even looking up. He was there to teach them something he had discovered, and he did not believe in wasting time.

What he had to say was, as we know, somewhat depressing: he informed his audiences that they had virtually no free will, that they were made up of hundreds of little 'I's', and that they were actually asleep. Yet this sweeping and oversimplified doctrine – rather like a non-political Marxism – created an effect of revelation. One member of his audience was a Jungian psychologist named Maurice Nicoll. He rushed home from his first Ouspensky lecture to tell his wife, still recovering from having their first baby: 'You must come and hear Ouspensky. He is the only man who has ever answered my questions.' Nicoll appeared to be 'irradiated by an inner light', and did not even ask to see the baby. As a result of his contact with Ouspensky, he broke with Jung, who had hoped that Nicoll would be his chief exponent in London.

It was Nicoll who talked to his friend Kenneth Walker, Hunterian Professor at the Royal College of Surgeons, who had just written a children's book about Noah's Ark. Gurdjieff's ideas, he said, represented a kind of Noah's Ark in the modern flood of violence and unbelief. Walker, as we have seen, felt that the atmosphere at Ouspensky's lecture was a little like the Presbyterian churches of his childhood. But he was also impressed by the scientific precision of Ouspensky's mind, and the lack of the usual idealistic waffle about Spirit, Love and so on. (One 'occultist', A.E. Waite, walked out, indignantly saying, 'Mr Ouspensky, there is no love in your system.') By now, Ouspensky's lectures had moved to 38 Warwick Gardens, Lady Rothermere having – inevitably – grown bored with the Work.

Gurdjieff, in the meantime, had failed to find the security he was looking for. He had left Constantinople for Germany, first for Berlin, then for Hellerau, near Dresden, where he hoped to take over the buildings left empty by the original Jacques Dalcroze Institute. They were owned by a man called Harold Dohrn, and parts were already let out to a smaller version of the Dalcroze Institute, to the Progressive schoolmaster A.S. Neill, and to another German headmaster named Karl Baer. But Gurdjieff wanted the whole place, and seems to have persuaded Dohrn to lease it to him. Neill and Baer naturally objected, and since they had signed leases, they had a strong case. Dohrn changed his mind, and when, according to Neill, Gurdjieff took him to court, protested that Gurdjieff had hypnotized him into agreeing to let him lease the whole building. Gurdjieff apparently lost the case. His biographer James Webb thinks it highly probable that he did use his hypnotic powers, in spite of the fact that, according to *Life is Real Only Then, When 'I Am'*, he had renounced them some time before 1910 because they retarded his spiritual progress. This is not to suggest that Gurdjieff stared into Dohrn's eyes like Svengali and ordered him to go to sleep. The 'telepathic' episode in Finland described by Ouspensky makes it clear that he knew how to build up a level of heightened vitality and to use it to establish some kind of direct influence over others.

Gurdjieff acquired some of Dalcroze's best pupils, but he still had no institute. So, in 1922, he went to London and gave a talk to Ouspensky's students. Ouspensky had never made any secret of the fact that the ideas were not his own, but had originated with Gurdjieff. So there was considerable excitement when it was learned that the Master himself was coming to see them. His first talk was on 13 February, 1922. Gurdjieff had now shaven his head, so that he looked stranger and more Asiatic than ever. Ouspensky's English was heavily accented, but more or less accurate; Gurdjieff's was purely functional, and he spoke in a kind of shorthand. When one lady asked what it would be like to be conscious in essence, he replied expressively: 'Everything more vivid.' At this first talk he emphasized the way we all become more 'mechanical' as we get older, and how, consequently, tremendous effort is needed to generate new energy.

At a later lecture he spoke briefly about man's many 'I's' and inability to govern the emotions. Then, after speaking for barely five minutes, he began to take questions. This was, in fact, one of his favourite methods, for he believed that mere talk may simply fail to penetrate, while individual questions revealed what his listeners really wanted to know. (Ouspensky came to adopt the same method.) On this occasion, he made the important comment that the chief cause of our weakness is 'our inability to apply our will to all three of our centres simultaneously'. He gave an example of how the total will might be applied to the moving centre – that a prisoner whose only chance of escape depended upon throwing a note written on a ball of paper through a high and inaccessible window would concentrate his whole being to make sure he succeeded. But the real problem was to apply the same will to all three centres – physical, intellectual and emotional – at the same time.

Orage, who was present, was even more deeply impressed with Gurdjieff than with Ouspensky. In fact, he now saw that Ouspensky had intellectualized Gurdjieff's teaching, and therefore, in a sense, 'falsified' it.

It was now Gurdjieff's ambition to open his institute in London. But he had reckoned without his reputation as a Russian spy. He was interviewed by the security services, and their verdict on him seems to have been unfavourable. (There is, in fact, some evidence that he had worked for the Russian Secret Service in Tibet.) In spite of the testimony of a committee of doctors – including Nicoll and Walker – before the Home Secretary, Gurdjieff's application to move to London was refused. Even Lady Rothermere's influence failed to do him any good. So he packed his bags – undoubtedly to Ouspensky's relief – and left for Paris. There he quickly found an ideal site for the Institute for the Harmonious Development of Man near Fontainebleau; it was a château called the Prieuré des Basses Loges, some 40 miles from Paris. It had formerly been the home of Madame de Maintenon, second wife of Louis XIV. Gurdjieff had no money, but Ouspensky raised it for him, with a large contribution from Lady Rothermere, so that he was able to lease the Priory for a year, with an option to buy. He sent for his pupils – who were still waiting in Berlin – and flung himself into violent activity to make money. Selling carpets would probably be less profitable than in Russia, so Gurdjieff leased two restaurants, went into the oil business, and set up as a psychiatrist specializing in drug addiction and alcoholism. (He seems to have had considerable success in this field although, regrettably, we lack details.)

Ouspensky came to Paris to offer help. While he was away, rumours began to circulate among his London pupils about Gurdjieff's tendency to seduce his female students. With typical loyalty, Ouspensky wrote to Orage to ask him to squash these rumours.

Orage himself had already decided to go and join Gurdjieff. After listening to the Master's talks, he felt as if he had received a religious Call. He was becoming tired of being an editor – since pre-war days the circulation of *The New Age* had slumped – and of the London literary scene. When he called on Ouspensky in the autumn of 1922 to ask his advice, Ouspensky, who had been watching Orage from the window of his flat, replied with typical brevity: 'I can see you have

already made up your mind, so why ask me?' And so began
the exodus from London which would also include Nicoll and
his fellow doctor James Young. John Bennett, back from
Constantinople, would also become a regular weekend visitor
at the Priory.

Orage must have wondered whether he had jumped out of
the frying pan into the fire. In the seven years since he had
met Ouspensky, Gurdjieff had ceased to rely on verbal
teaching to convey his message; he was looking for some form
of 'action'. Even in Petrograd he had recognized that the
discipline required by dancing could help his students to unite
the three centres. The deliberate hardships and privations –
beyond the demands of the situation – that he had imposed
upon the disciples who followed him to the Caucasus had
strengthened his belief in the efficacy of 'super-effort'. His
discovery of Dalcroze's method suggested an extension of the
Eastern dances he had presented in Tiflis in *The Struggle of the
Magicians*. So had the 'Stop!' exercise. So at last Gurdjieff had
a system of physical exercises to offer, as well as a system of
ideas. And the starting point was super-effort.

When Orage arrived at the Priory, he was first of all told not
to smoke – which 'almost killed him' – then handed a spade
and told to dig. The day began around 4 a.m. with a light
breakfast of coffee and rolls. Then he was made to dig until
evening. Orage did not even have the consolation that it was
useful work that would improve the Priory; sometimes
Gurdjieff made his followers dig a ditch one day and fill it in
the next. Orage, although tall, was an overweight man, and
he was soon in such a state of exhaustion that he often found
himself in tears. Then one day at the end of five months, 'in
the depths of despair' and feeling he could go on no longer,
he decided to make one more extra effort. To his
astonishment, he suddenly began enjoying the digging. And
Gurdjieff, who had been observing him from a distance,
suddenly said: 'Now Orage, I think you dig enough – let us
go and drink coffee.' For he had other plans for Orage than
growing vegetables. His experience with Ouspensky had
shown him the value of 'intellectual' pupils. Orage was to be

Ouspensky's replacement as his chief propagandist.

On 13 December, 1923, Gurdjieff's followers gave the first public performance in the West of the 'movements', at the Champs Elysées Theatre, and although reviews were mixed, it made a considerable impact. Orage was not present; together with Dr Stoerneval he was on his way to New York to further Gurdjieff's ambition to conquer the world.

Meanwhile, back in Warwick Gardens, Ouspensky was teaching Gurdjieff's ideas in his own way – intellectually. Inevitably, he laid enormous emphasis on the cosmology – the ray of creation, the Law of Three, the Law of Seven and the Enneagram. With his thick glasses and dry manner, he was not capable of inspiring the same fascination and devotion as the Master in Paris, yet his students gradually found that he was becoming an addiction. In *Venture with Ideas*, Kenneth Walker has recorded how, to begin with, he found Ouspensky interesting and original, but felt no compulsion to go to every meeting. Little by little, as he tested Ouspensky's ideas about lack of self-awareness, he began to feel an increasing compulsion to return; finally, he reached the stage where Ouspensky's lectures were the most important thing in his life. He was particularly impressed by his comments about 'wastage'. We all have a certain amount of energy to carry us through the day; but we waste so much in useless activities and negative emotions that we have no chance of having energy left over for personal evolution. Walker discovered:

The more I put into practice the psychological principles of the System, the more convinced I became of their value. I found, for example, that with their help I was able to overcome certain difficulties in my professional life, difficulties resulting from negative imagination. I no longer lay awake at night, as I formerly did, listening for the telephone to ring and for the night-sister to tell me that the patient on whom I had operated had suddenly collapsed. I ceased to wonder during the small hours of the morning whether it would not have been better for me to have done this rather than that, for by now I had fully realised the futility of such thoughts. And as the wastage of energy through worry and identification lessened I found myself able to do more and with steadily increasing efficiency.

After publication of *A New Model of the Universe* in 1931, the number of Ouspensky's pupils began to increase. Soon there were so many that he had to hold two meetings a week. New faces continued to appear, but many of them dropped out almost immediately. One Spiritualist who asked Ouspensky his views on life 'on the other side' was offended when Ouspensky replied that it was far more important to study life on this side. Another man was upset because Ouspensky brushed aside his attempt to translate the ideas of the System into religious terminology, and also failed to return. Ouspensky did not mind in the least. In fact, he explained that one of the major principles of the Work was 'artificially produced friction', and that this often involved irritating everybody. Gurdjieff himself constantly applied this method at the Priory, even to setting his pupils against one another.

As for Ouspensky, his students noticed that he no longer went to see Gurdjieff in Paris. There had been a total break, no one knew why. Ouspensky's old friend Mouraviev tells a story of how, when asked about this break, Ouspensky replied: 'If someone close to you, your near relative, turned out to be a criminal, what would you do?' This sounds like more than an intellectual disagreement, and the likelihood is that Ouspensky had received confirmation of the rumours about seduction that he had ordered Orage to suppress.

When Ouspensky visited New York many years later, he was asked again about the break with Gurdjieff, and replied simply that when he had discovered that 'Gurdjieff was wrong', he had to leave him. But since Ouspensky continued to teach a system that was basically Gurdjieff's, it is hard to understand what he meant by the assertion that Gurdjieff was wrong.

The obvious difference between Ouspensky's 'method' and Gurdjieff's is that Ouspensky's was much gentler: it did not consist of trying to bring people to a point of 'second wind' by driving them to near exhaustion. Yet Ouspensky himself came to feel that more actual 'work' was required. In 1933, the group decided to acquire a house, and a suitable property was found at Hayes, on the Great West Road out of London. Here the assorted group of professional men and women did physical work – gardening, woodwork, housework – but the aim was largely self-observation. Walker has a delightful story of two of them being sent out to beat carpets. His approach was simple – raise the carpet off the ground with one hand and beat it with the other. His companion wanted to suspend the carpet from a line, and spent a long time finding a suitable clothesline and stringing it between two trees. It proved to be too low and had to be raised. After a series of vicissitudes that sound like *Three Men in a Boat*, they finally started to beat the carpet, and the rope snapped. It can be seen why Ouspensky's students seem to have enjoyed the process of getting to know themselves through self-observation.

Ouspensky explained that one of the main problems with civilized human beings is their 'false personalities', the front they have built up to meet the world. 'Madame Ouspensky', who seems to have been in many ways a stronger character than her husband, had an eagle eye for weakness, and a deadly gift for mimicry. Walker describes her imitations of 'Mr N.' arriving late for lunch and hoping no one had noticed, 'Miss D.' dusting a room as if applying powder to her nose, 'Mr M.' grinding coffee beans with as much effort as he would put into raising a heavy bucket from a deep well. She also had a gift of words – most of them in Russian – and had no hesitation in making remarks like 'You are a warning to us all and quite useless' or describing someone's conversation as 'pouring emptiness into a void'. She likened the 'false personality' to a huge hot-air pie which the owner carried about on a tray in order to be admired, but which had to be treated very carefully, or its thin crust would be damaged.

All this, Walker explains, developed in them the ability to laugh at themselves and at one another, and made for a relaxed and happy atmosphere.

Madame Ouspensky differed from her husband in having

a strong religious bent, and so spent much time arranging readings from world scriptures – the sayings of the Buddha, the *Bhagavad Gita*, texts of Taoism and Sufism, even the Church Fathers. And Ouspensky, who had always insisted that the Fourth Way should be regarded as a scientific method, seems to have accepted all this without protest. According to his own doctrine of sleep and mechanicalness, religious readings should have been useless, a method of self-deception. The fact that he accepted them seems to indicate that he acknowledged that the world's great religions have fundamentally the same aim as the Work. On the other hand, the mystery may be explained simply by the fact that Madame Ouspensky had preferred to be at the Priory with Gurdjieff rather than in London with her husband, and that Gurdjieff's attitude to religion was quite unlike Ouspensky's. When Gurdjieff finally sent her away, she came to England with the deepest reluctance, and she and Ouspensky continued to live separately. (In *The Harmonious Circle*, James Webb records that Ouspensky had a mistress.)

Within three years, Ouspensky's community had become so successful that they decided they needed a larger place, and moved to a house at Virginia Water, near Ascot. But this had disadvantages; Lyne Place was so large that the atmosphere of intimacy was lost, and they felt they belonged to an institution. They also saw less of the Ouspenskys. But they moved a step further in the direction of the Priory by felling timber, building a sawmill, and farming on a larger scale. And after a few years, Ouspensky went still further in Gurdjieff's direction by introducing training in 'the movements'. 'Head, body, arms and legs often moved in different rhythms and when it seemed natural to turn in a certain direction the exercise often dictated that one should turn in the opposite direction,' according to Walker. He goes on:

It was difficult at the end of a hard day's work in London to drive out some twenty odd miles into the country in order to take part in these supremely difficult exercises. At such times the flimsiest excuse seemed to provide a valid reason for not

going. A whole conversation would start up inside me; the fog
was getting thicker . . . next day would be a heavy day . . . But
the strange thing was that however fatigued I might be when
I began Gurdjieff's difficult exercises I always drove back to
London so full of energy that I had no desire to go to bed.

But Ouspensky now recognized that the sheer success of his
enterprise had become his main problem. 'He could either cut
down the size of the group and carry on more intensive work
with a smaller following, or else he could open the door wider
and allow more people to enter.' The latter course, which
might seem self-defeating, was the one they chose. Instead of
the Warwick Gardens flat (which they had kept on), they
would find a larger house in London. One was eventually
found in Hammersmith. But with the war approaching, the
Ouspenskys apparently decided that they needed some
innocent 'cover'. Why this should be so is not clear, and it
seems likely that it was a hangover from the old days of
'secrecy', when the notion that they were a secret society
formed an additional bond. (In fact, Ouspensky *was* under
Home Office surveillance in the late '30s as a potential Russian
agent, but was not even aware of it.) At all events, the group
decided to call themselves the Historico-Psychological Society,
and claim to be studying Eastern religions. They would even
present public lectures on 'appropriate subjects', and impart
their real purpose only to members of the audience who
seemed suitable . . .

While Ouspensky had been building up his own secure
following in England, Gurdjieff's group had been through
some strange vicissitudes. Throughout the inter-war years
Gurdjieff's main problem was money. Ouspensky built up a
following of well-off disciples who could afford to pay for their
instruction; Gurdjieff had a large group of Russians who
needed to be supported. He drove himself so hard during the
early days of the Priory that one night, driving back from
Paris, he was unable to stay awake. He pulled his car into the
side of the road, and was awakened the next morning when
a farm wagon tried to get past. His night in the open led to

a chill whose effects were long lasting.

Then malicious gossip was caused by the death of the writer Katherine Mansfield at the Priory in January 1924. She was rumoured to have been worked to death by the demonic 'magician'. In fact, she had arrived there – in October 1923 – already dying of tuberculosis. Gurdjieff had the curious idea of placing her bed over a barn where she could smell the odour of cows, but it did no good; she died after an evening of watching the Gurdjieff dances.

By that time, Orage was in New York preparing the way for Gurdjieff's arrival. He disembarked towards the end of December, and was taken to a bookshop on 44th St, whose part-owner promptly fell in love with him. A few days later, Orage gave his first lecture, explaining to his audience that Gurdjieff had been a member of a group called the Seekers after Truth, who had spent years searching for esoteric knowledge in the East, and had brought back its secrets to the West. There was an element of truth in this, but it seems almost certain that the Seekers after Truth were a product of Gurdjieff's imagination.

In early January 1924, Gurdjieff arrived, together with the Hartmanns and other followers. A first performance of the sacred dances was given in a small hall whose stage had been reconstructed by the group. It was free, and Gurdjieff himself handed out tickets in the foyer, scrutinizing the faces of the people and ignoring some of them. In early February there was a performance at the Neighbourhood Playhouse; it lasted for four hours, and left the audience deeply impressed. In addition to the dances, Gurdjieff's pupils demonstrated certain 'magic' tricks involving telepathy. A pupil in the audience would take some object from a member of the audience, and 'transmit' it to someone on stage, who would accurately describe it. The names of operas were also 'transmitted', and Hartmann would then play extracts from them on the piano. 'Pictures' were 'transmitted' to the artist de Salzmann, who drew them on large sheets of paper. Gurdjieff explained – through Orage – that some of these demonstrations were 'tricks', some were 'half-tricks', and some were genuine psychical phenomena; but he left it to the audience to guess which was which. One young man named Stanley Nott confessed himself totally baffled. The writer Llewellyn Powys said that the pupils were like a hutchful of hypnotized rabbits, while another commentator described Gurdjieff as looking like a riding master.

But in the novelty-hungry America of the jazz age, this search for salvation through self-knowledge made only a temporary impact, and audiences declined. A trip to Chicago – at the invitation of the Diaghilev choreographer Adolf Bolm – was a success, as was a final performance at Carnegie Hall. But financially, the trip was not as successful as Gurdjieff had hoped.

Then, in July 1924, it suddenly looked as if Gurdjieff's interesting career had been prematurely terminated. He was driving back from Paris to the Priory when his car crashed into a tree; he was found lying on his back beside it. Doctors diagnosed serious concussion. (Ouspensky, who visited the Priory during this period, believed that Gurdjieff was being punished by higher powers for his transgressions.) When Gurdjieff finally recovered, he announced that he had decided to close down the Priory, and most of the Russians left. Gurdjieff himself, apparently determined to transmit his ideas to posterity, began to write the first series of *All and Everything, Beelzebub's Tales to his Grandson*, a work that became famed for its impenetrability and for the weirdness of its neologisms.

In *The Harmonious Circle*, James Webb makes the interesting suggestion that Gurdjieff arranged his own accident. He points out that Gurdjieff showed no outward sign of having been in a car crash. He was found lying beside the car with his head on a cushion. When brought back from the hospital, he was unconscious for five days, yet his fist clenched violently when Madame de Hartmann took his pulse. He is also reported to have told his attendants where to massage him.

The accident itself is a mystery. That day, Gurdjieff's car had been in the garage for its steering column to be checked. It seems odd that the steering column should then have failed – although perhaps credible enough for anyone with experience of garages. However, also that day, Gurdjieff's secretary Olga de Hartmann had been given power of attorney, and told to return to the Priory by train, instead of – as usual – in Gurdjieff's car. She was irritated, since it was a hot day, and she would have preferred to travel in the open car. She was also puzzled when Gurdjieff cancelled an appointment at the last moment; he was normally thoughtful when dealing with people outside the Work. At the time of the crash, at about 4.30 in the afternoon, she was awakened from a doze by Gurdjieff's voice calling her name. Since we know Gurdjieff possessed telepathic powers, could this not also have been part of the plan?

If Webb is correct, what could have been the purpose of such a deception? The answer may be that Gurdjieff was sick of being the 'circus master' and guru. His power to fascinate and arouse devotion made him the slave of his own disciples. He had already behaved in a similar manner in Russia when he had abruptly announced the dissolution of the group. Before the accident, he spent two days a week in Paris, and he may often have wished it could have been more. After all, in London, Ouspensky lived quietly in his flat, and gave lectures once a week. In France, Gurdjieff spent most of his time in the midst of his disciples, or trying to make money to support them.

The accident certainly changed all that. Large numbers of followers left the Priory – particularly the Russians, who were the biggest drain on Gurdjieff's resources. Olga de Hartmann took over the running of the place. Gurdjieff had told them: 'All my life I have lived for others. Now I will live for myself a while.'

How does Webb's theory explain the fact that Gurdjieff's hands *were* lacerated, and that many of his followers were shocked by the change in him? The obvious possibility is that, in faking his accident, Gurdjieff failed to jump out of the car quickly enough.

What shocked the disciples was not so much that Gurdjieff

had had an accident as that, according to his own teaching, he should have been 'beyond' the law of accident. He possessed 'essence', and essence is subject to the laws of destiny, not accident.

But whether Gurdjieff's car crash was accident, destiny or play-acting, it undoubtedly freed him from the trap that had closed around him. After 1924, the Priory was suddenly a quieter place.

Six

'There is no System'

ONE OF our main sources for Ouspensky's final years is Stanley Nott, the young Englishman who had been introduced to Gurdjieff's teaching through Orage. In *Journey through this World: The Second Journal of a Pupil*, Nott described a visit to Ouspensky in London in the spring of 1935. He had seen Ouspensky only once before and, on that occasion had, like most people, found him rather cold and detached; now he was surprised to find him a warm and friendly man. But Madame Ouspensky proved to be a dragon, and at one point Nott had to remonstrate: 'I didn't come here to be put through a catechism, but to have a friendly conversation.' Nott lent Ouspensky a copy of the typescript of *Beelzebub's Tales*, about which he was obviously intensely curious. Nott regarded it as a kind of Bible. Ouspensky agreed to allow Nott to attend one of his groups – he told him that he now had more than 1,000 pupils – on condition that he did not talk about *Beelzebub*. But after a few glasses of wine he began to relax and unburden himself on the subject of Gurdjieff:

You know, when Gurdjieff started his Institute in Paris I did everything I could for him. I raised money for him and sent him pupils, many of them influential people. When he bought the Prieuré I went there myself and Madame stayed for some time. But I found that he had changed from when I knew him in Russia. He was difficult in Essentuki and Constantinople but more so in Fontainebleau. His behaviour had changed. He did many things that I did not like, but it wasn't what he did that upset me, it was the stupid way he did them. He came to London to my group and made things very unpleasant for me. After this I saw that I must break with him . . .

He went on to say that he was convinced that Gurdjieff had 'lost contact with the source' after Essentuki, and that he had never recovered from his car accident. Nott denied this, but could see that nothing he could say would alter Ouspensky's opinion. 'I began to see traces of the inflexible mental attitude that besets Russians . . . once they have adopted a mental attitude to a given situation they will stick to it, whatever the cost.'

According to Nott, the break had come after a visit from Gurdjieff to Ouspensky's London group in 1922 (when Gurdjieff was accompanied by Pinder). Gurdjieff had told Ouspensky that he was too intellectual, and was working on the wrong lines. If he wished to *understand* he must stop and start to work with Gurdjieff again . . . Understandably, Ouspensky rejected this – after being in the Work for seven years he must have felt that he understood it as well as he ever would. In a sense he was right; and the point is underlined by the fact that he handed Nott the typescript of *The Strange Life of Ivan Osokin*, which he had been revising. Ouspensky had already surrendered enough of his individuality to Gurdjieff.

Nott, of course, had no doubt whatever that Gurdjieff's outbursts of rudeness and eccentricity were carefully calculated to bring enlightenment to his pupils, and the memoirs of some of these pupils – like Fritz Peters – make it clear he was fundamentally correct. Yet, as we have seen, it is also clear that he failed to recognize that Ouspensky possessed his own kind of genius, and that he was right to wish to go his own way. An Ouspensky who returned to Gurdjieff as a disciple would have been emasculated.

At the first meeting Nott attended, Ouspensky arrived half an hour or so late, after an advanced pupil had already asked the audience for questions. Then Ouspensky answered the questions one by one. 'As the evening went on,' says Nott, 'I became more and more impressed with the breadth and clarity of his massive and powerful mind – so far as *knowledge* was concerned.' Nott continued to feel, however, that Ouspensky was missing Gurdjieff's basic point.

Nevertheless, as they shared glasses of red wine, Nott began to feel 'a real affection' for Ouspensky. The problem, he saw, was that Ouspensky wanted to 'come to an understanding' with Gurdjieff – and that was impossible. You either accepted Gurdjieff as a teacher or you didn't. The two attitudes – Ouspensky's and Nott's – were incompatible. Ouspensky felt that knowledge was an objective fact, like a mathematical table; a teacher might be useful as a catalyst, but in the ultimate sense, no teacher is 'necessary'. He obviously felt that Nott's tendency to accept Gurdjieff as an infallible guru was a sign of a feeble intellect.

Yet in spite of his success as a teacher, Ouspensky's dissatisfaction with his own progress was plain. He told Nott one day that it was now necessary to get in touch with 'an esoteric school'. 'There must be schools, either in Europe or the Near East.' In effect, he was back at square one.

Gurdjieff's comment, when Nott told him that he liked Ouspensky, was: 'Ouspensky very nice man to talk to and drink vodka with, but he is weak man.'

Reflecting on this later, Nott concluded that Ouspensky's weakness lay in his emotional centre. Intellectuals – like Shaw and Bertrand Russell – are particularly prone to this: '. . . one expects them to be adult emotionally, and they are not.'

The point is underlined by Nott's story of Ouspensky's comment when Nott asked him if he had read the typescript of *Beelzebub*: 'No, it sticks in my throat.' *Beelzebub* is, admittedly, an infuriatingly obscure book. Yet Ouspensky's failure to try to get to grips with it reveals that his remarkable intellect was hobbled by pride and touchiness.

In spite of their disagreements, Gurdjieff continued to feel kindly towards the Ouspenskys, and sent them parcels of delicacies every time Nott returned to London from the Prieuré. One day, Madame Ouspensky asked Nott what he got from Gurdjieff. His answer is significant:

Mr Gurdjieff says things to me about myself which hit me right in my feelings, in my essence, so that I can never forget them; and little by little the effect is to change something in me and give me more understanding of myself and other people; at the same time it is accompanied by a realisation of how little I actually do understand. Mr Ouspensky appeals to my mind and I'm never tired of listening to him. But this doesn't change things in myself. I think I can say that I get more for inner work from one lunch with Mr Gurdjieff than from a year of Mr Ouspensky's groups.

Oddly enough, Madame Ouspensky replied: 'Yes, I think I know what you mean.'

Another story of Nott's makes the point even more powerfully. In the second half of the 1930s he was depressed by the rise of the Nazis, and by setbacks in his personal life – including an accident in which his son lost a leg. He went to see Gurdjieff in Paris, and after lunch, Gurdjieff asked him into his sitting-room. Then Gurdjieff sat at the harmonium and began to play, 'keeping his eyes fixed on me with a look of deep compassion and power'.

Little by little I became aware that he was conveying something to me both through the music – the combination of the notes – and by the telepathic means which he understood so well. A change began to take place in me; I began to understand something, and a feeling of conscious hope and conscious faith began to displace the dark hopeless depression.

When he left, 'a healing of the psychic wounds had begun'.

Back in London, Ouspensky was lecturing to crowded audiences in Hammersmith. But Madame Ouspensky had become seriously ill. To Nott's astonishment, Ouspensky decided that Gurdjieff was the only one who could do anything for her. And in spite of Ouspensky's comment that he felt Gurdjieff had now lost touch with the 'source', Nott agreed to try to persuade Gurdjieff to come to England – Madame Ouspensky being too ill to go to Paris.

With typical generosity, Gurdjieff instantly agreed to come

to London. But two days before he was due to arrive, war broke out. Fortunately, Madame Ouspensky seems to have made some kind of recovery without his help.

As soon as the air raids began, it became difficult to carry on with meetings in London, and petrol rationing and the black-out made Virginia Water inaccessible. On 4 January, 1941, Madame Ouspensky sailed for America with a small group of 'the faithful', and two weeks later, Ouspensky followed her. It had been almost 21 years since he had received the letter from Claude Bragdon with the royalty cheque for *Tertium Organum*, and the two decades since then had been a period of peace and prosperity. Now, just as it began to look as if his work was entering a new phase of success, he was once again being condemned to exile.

The voyage took more than six weeks – the *Georgic* had to go far out of its way to dodge U-boats – and they arrived in early March. Madame Ouspensky had taken a house at Rumson, on the coast of New Jersey. Stanley Nott, who had been in America a year, was glad to see that she now looked much better, and was also friendlier and less forbidding. Nott soon went to have lunch with Ouspensky in a New York hotel, and suggested that he should come and address the 'Orage group', of which he had become a member.

Orage himself had been dead since November 1934. Unlike Ouspensky, he never renounced Gurdjieff: Gurdjieff renounced him. While Orage was on a trip to England in 1930, Gurdjieff had taken over his New York group and made the members sign a letter in which they renounced Orage. Typically, Orage lost no time in signing it too. Exactly why Gurdjieff turned against Orage is unclear. He may have felt that, like Ouspensky, Orage was carrying the Work in the wrong direction. Or he may simply have decided that everybody needed a 'shock'. The shock seems to have done Orage no harm; he returned to England and devoted himself to the curious ideas of Major Clifford Douglas on 'Social Credit' – a system designed to replace money with a kind of barter. And in spite of Gurdjieff's prohibition, Orage's group continued to regard him with reverence.

Ouspensky attended a meeting of the group at a house in Madison Avenue, and was oddly unimpressive. 'No authority,' said one of Orage's pupils. They knew Gurdjieff and felt that Ouspensky had neither Gurdjieff's fire nor Orage's warmth and brilliance. The Ouspensky group that subsequently formed had only about 50 members, and by the end of two years, only half a dozen remained. On the other hand, many of Ouspensky's former pupils from England decided to join him in America, and for this group, Ouspensky, not Gurdjieff, was the Master.

Yet Nott, who saw something of Ouspensky in New York, felt that he had lost the old drive. Nott attributes this to the infirmities of age, but in fact Ouspensky was only 63. The real problem was almost certainly that he had been uprooted once too often. He was drinking too much – Nott says that he was imbibing strong concoctions that required a stomach of iron – and obviously felt that he had simply not achieved the inner freedom he had set out to attain. By nature, he was a gentle romantic, whose attempts to turn himself into a kind of scientific guru were an affront to his fundamental nature. He told Nott that his strong potations were 'the only thing that relieves the boredom and depression that comes over me at times'.

In fact, Ouspensky's alcoholism provides us with a vital clue. The immediate effect of alcohol – particularly spirits – is 'uplift', an increase of 'inner pressure'. It is as if one has closed certain inner valves and ceased to 'leak'. 'Depression' means, literally, low pressure. Now any form of purposeful activity has the effect of closing the leaks and raising our inner pressure. For romantic intellectuals of Ouspensky's type, the best possible remedy for depression is creative thinking or writing. But Ouspensky had ceased to do any original thinking many years ago. *Tertium Organum* and *A New Model of the Universe* lay decades behind him. He had learned to achieve his 'intellectual feedback' through other people; he was at his best lecturing to an audience. It brought out the 'iron man', the scientist, the psychologist. But when he was alone, he had a sense of anticlimax. There was 'nothing to do'.

These were the times when he enjoyed relaxing with friends like Nott, or his new disciple Rodney Collin (who had travelled over on the same boat), and reminiscing nostalgically about St Petersburg. But if there was no one to talk to, he seems to have become subject to depression. It was at about this time – in 1942 – that he wrote to Bennett that man's only hope is to work with the higher emotional centres, and added gloomily: 'And we do not know how this is to be done.'

Ouspensky had now turned his back completely on Gurdjieff. When Nott told him that Gurdjieff might be moving to New York, he replied that in that case he would go to California. Nott was asked to take an active part in Ouspensky's New York group, but felt unable to do so because he would not have been allowed to mention Gurdjieff or *Beelzebub's Tales*.

In the autumn of 1942, the Ouspenskys acquired a new 'headquarters' – a vast house called Franklin Farms in Mendham, New Jersey. It had 300 acres of land, and when the Notts paid a visit, it struck them as a re-creation of Lyne Place – in fact, many of the people *were* the same. There was also something of the same air of regimentation – pupils were not allowed to address one another by their Christian names, and Nott was again forbidden to mention Gurdjieff. He and his wife taught Gurdjieff's dances there, but he was not even allowed to reply to questions about their creator. When, on 7 December, 1941, the Japanese bombed Pearl Harbour and America entered the war, Ouspensky was probably relieved that Gurdjieff would not now be returning to torment him.

At Franklin Farms, Madame Ouspensky became increasingly the dominant force; Ouspensky often sat apart, silently drinking wine. Madame had become more despotic than ever, and the tap of her stick made the pupils look at one another nervously. One of them compared her to Gurdjieff – but she seems to have lacked the Master's kindness. Nott was one of the few who had the courage to stand up to her: before leaving Mendham to teach at a progressive school in Vermont, he shocked her by telling her that trying to teach 'the System' without mentioning Gurdjieff was like trying to teach Christianity without mentioning Jesus Christ.

Ouspensky's depression was making him increasingly bad tempered. When a new edition of *A New Model of the Universe* appeared with a blurb stating that Ouspensky was working in a group with Gurdjieff near London, he flew into a rage and proposed to call a press conference. Nott tried to persuade New York editors to send representatives and discovered – not surprisingly – that no one was remotely interested. And when Ouspensky heard that Bennett was teaching the System in England, he wrote him an angry letter pointing out that he had been sworn to secrecy. Visitors to Mendham heard Bennett described as a plagiarist and a thief.

When Nott returned to Mendham after a year in Vermont, he found conditions relatively unchanged. Madame Ouspensky as bossy as ever, and as paranoid about Gurdjieff. It was this that led to his decision to leave. He had been invited to dinner by a couple he had known for years, pupils of Ouspensky. They began to ask him about *Beelzebub's Tales*, and since they were dining at the couple's home, Nott felt free to talk about it, telling them that it was 'the Bible of the Work'. When they asked where they could get hold of it, he referred them to Madame Ouspensky.

The next day he was summoned by Madame, who accused him of breaking his promise. Nott replied that he had kept his promise not to discuss Gurdjieff at Franklin Farms, but when he was elsewhere he felt free to do as he liked. She described this as mere quibbling. Nott then pointed out firmly that she was teaching Gurdjieff's System at Mendham. Madame Ouspensky became angry, and Nott ended by telling her that her pupils were all stuck at the 'mi' level, and that if they were to progress to 'fa', they would need a shock – the kind of shock that could be provided by Gurdjieff and his book. This was the end. Nott announced he was leaving and they shook hands; he never saw her or Ouspensky again. In his second *Journal of a Pupil*, Nott states his considered opinion that after Ouspensky cut himself off from Gurdjieff, his work began to lose its value.

He was probably right. Yet it is equally clear that Ouspensky could not have remained with Gurdjieff. Gurdjieff needed disciples, and Ouspensky, for all his weakness, was too big a man to be anyone's disciple forever. The dilemma was insoluble.

What seems very clear is that Ouspensky had lost his mainspring. He felt he had reached a dead end. He had caught his glimpses of freedom, of the higher emotional centres; now he felt stuck in everyday reality, too old for further mental effort. Towards the end of the war, he seems to have thought constantly about returning to England. One reason was probably the increasing dominance of Madame Ouspensky at Mendham. She was suffering from Parkinson's Disease, and it seems to have made her even more domineering. Nevertheless, Ouspensky was not ignored – on the contrary, some of his pupils were inclined to worship him. One woman who fell on her knees before him was sternly told to get up at once and never do it again. Even his habit of sitting silent as he boozed was interpreted as a teaching gambit. It must have struck him as ironic to be regarded with so much reverence when he felt that he had lost all the answers. When his step-daughter asked him for advice on how to combat her depression, he could only snap: 'Pray, Lenotchka, pray!'

In spite, however, of his indignation with Bennett, Ouspensky himself was now thinking of publishing something about the Work – a series of lectures he had given in England in the late 1930s. But he seems to have had difficulty finding a publisher, and the book, *The Psychology of Man's Possible Evolution*, was not issued until in 1950, after his death. During the war, Ouspensky was also engaged on the lengthy account of his years with Gurdjieff, 'Fragments of an Unknown Teaching', which, as already mentioned, was later published under the title *In Search of the Miraculous*.

Towards the end of the war, two English followers, who had been in charge of Lyne Place, made their way to Mendham. James Webb quotes them as saying that they found Ouspensky disabled 'as if by a stroke', and that he was virtually a prisoner. He asked them to try and get the

Hammersmith house back from the Navy (who had requisitioned it) and prepare it for his return.

Yet by the end of the war Ouspensky's health was so poor that there seemed doubt whether he would be able to cross the Atlantic. (He was suffering from a serious kidney complaint, exacerbated by his heavy drinking.) But he finally arrived – without his wife – in January 1947, and was driven straight to Lyne Place. Kenneth Walker comments that they hardly recognized him; he was 'a man on whom Death had already set its mark'. Ouspensky was deeply preoccupied, as if 'his mind was deeply engaged on some problem'. That problem, Walker thinks, was probably that of 'Eternal Recurrence', and the notion that he would have to return to live his life all over again – and try and do better next time.

A few weeks later, on 24 February, 1947, the 'Historico-Psychological Society' met at the hall in Colet Gardens. Ouspensky's English follower Dr Francis Roles had organized a large audience, but they were dismayed by Ouspensky's appearance and manner. He was hobbling on a cane, and looked old, bent and sick; his English seemed less comprehensible than ever. He used a kind of private secretary called Miss Quinn – from Mendham – to take questions, but he seemed impatient of most of them, and kept snapping: 'Be simpler' or 'Start from what you know'. When Kenneth Walker asked if he had abandoned the System, he shocked everyone by answering: 'There is no System'.

Walker gathered that Ouspensky had evolved some new plan for the Work in London, but could also see that he was too weak to carry it out. It seems possible that it was based on his idea that everyone should spend time remembering his life in detail, to fix it in memory for the next incarnation.

At the next two meetings, on 5 and 12 March, it became even clearer that Ouspensky had somehow lost his belief in the System. When people talked about being mechanical, he asked them who had told them so. He even dismissed self-remembering. When someone asked him how to find harmony, he replied: 'This is your question? This is my question now, and I have no answer'. He no longer believed in the possibility of change. To a lady who asked why he would not help them, he replied that he had no help to give.

But, interestingly enough, he told his pupils that they must have a straightforward, everyday aim, and that only by working alone could one make progress. This was a flat contradiction of Gurdjieff's teaching that nothing could be achieved by working alone. Was this a sign of Ouspensky's disillusionment, or was it, in fact, a new insight? There were three more meetings, and at the last – on 18 June – Ouspensky again emphasized the importance of the individual finding out what he or she wanted and then pursuing it. It was as if he recognized that 'enlightenment' should not be pursued for its own sake, but as a by-product of some other work. His own problem was that he *had* pursued it for its own sake, and now had no 'work' to do.

Clear evidence of his loss of direction and purpose is provided by the fact that he decided to return to America – an obviously retrogressive step. Then, at the last minute, when his pupils were all on board, ready to leave, he arrived in his wheelchair and announced that he had changed his mind. He was now behaving with the same lack of consideration of which he had accused Gurdjieff, although it is not clear whether this was intentional – to administer a 'shock' – or merely the result of illness.

Ouspensky spent much of his last months in England revisiting places associated with his past – evidently in an attempt to fix them in his mind for his next existence. On one occasion he decided not to get out of the car at Lyne, but sat in it all night, surrounded by cats. (He believed that cats are the only animals that possess astral bodies and that this is why witches use them as familiars.) One lady stood by the car, her arm raised in solemn salute.

But the end, after all, was not to be pathetic and anticlimactic. James Webb's researches into Ouspensky's last days reveal that his pupils were convinced that something strange had happened. Ouspensky seemed to become telepathic, to such an extent that people in attendance on him became worried, and asked him to use words to communicate. Lyne seemed 'full of presences', and when one day a powerful presence seemed to manifest itself, Ouspensky asked: 'You notice?' His pupils became convinced that he had achieved 'Cosmic Consciousness', and one of them described him as 'an angel'. Another witness said that 'what was going on was God's business', apparently meaning that supernatural forces were now intervening. Rodney Collin was to declare that he felt that a Christlike being was presiding over Ouspensky's death.

Collin seems to have taken it upon himself to try to make Ouspensky 'die consciously', and to make sure that he did not 'go gentle into that good night'. Others state that Ouspensky needed no encouragement, and spent his last days making 'super-efforts', even waking his pupils up in the middle of the night. It was, according to Collin, in his arms that Ouspensky finally died at dawn on 2 October, 1947, after dressing himself and summoning the household for a 'final briefing'. Not long before his death he had repeated: 'I abandon the System. Start again for yourselves.' He was buried in Lyne churchyard.

Collin retreated to the dressing-room next to Ouspensky's bedroom, and locked himself in for six days. When someone tried to climb up a ladder to look into the room, the window opened and Collin pushed the ladder to the ground. Finally, Collin rang the bell that Ouspensky rang when he needed attention. He was found sitting cross-legged on Ouspensky's bed, dirty and unshaven, and he asked his wife Janet to bring him lime juice. He later told her – and his sister-in-law, Joyce Collin-Smith – that he had been in communication with Ouspensky during all this period, and that the disclosures were so important that he was determined not to be disturbed. The result of this communication led him to formulate a theory of 'four worlds', each on different vibrational rates, and to write a book called *The Theory of Celestial Influence*.[1] He was to die, under mysterious circumstances, on 3 May, 1956, after falling from a tower in Mexico.

Now Ouspensky was dead, the faithful asked Madame Ouspensky what they were to do. To their amazement, she answered that they were to contact Gurdjieff in Paris. Gurdjieff himself wrote to Lyne: 'You are sheep without a shepherd; come to me.'

This caused consternation. Ouspensky's pupils had long ago accepted his assertion that Gurdjieff had lost his sense of direction after Essentuki and virtually gone mad – or, at least, gone bad. Contact with American pupils must have confirmed that impression: from the time Orage had formed his group there, Gurdjieff's demands for money had been unremitting; it looked as if he thought of his American disciples as sheep who were there to be fleeced. In fact, he seemed to be doing his best to alienate his pupils – in the book *Herald of Coming Good*, he claimed he had founded his Institute for 'purely personal ends'. Pupils deserted in droves – which may have been what he wanted.

The Priory had been sold in 1933, and Gurdjieff had retired to the Grand Hotel in Paris. From 1933 to mid-1935 he had lived in America, where he was hoping to re-establish an institute. But fate seemed against him. D.H. Lawrence's ex-disciple Mabel Dodge Luhan changed her mind about allowing him to set it up at Taos, in New Mexico. Then another disciple, Jean Toomer, tried to arrange a meeting with an American senator, but the senator's plane exploded in mid-air. Gurdjieff even tried to return to Russia, but was turned down by the Soviet authorities. He returned to Paris – via Germany – in the late summer of 1935, and soon had another enthusiastic group around him. In 1936, he moved into 6 rue des Colonels Renard, in the Russian quarter, north of the Etoile. At this period, the old, formidable Gurdjieff, who had reminded an American critic of a riding master or a circus ringmaster, and whom de Salzmann had called a demon, gave way to a gentler and more kindly person. When the war came, Gurdjieff stayed on in Paris, and the occupying Germans seem to have regarded him as a mild and harmless old man. [2]

About half the Lyne group decided to follow Madame Ouspensky's advice, and exactly a year after Ouspensky's death, on 2 October, 1948, Kenneth Walker and his wife Mary arrived in Paris. They arrived at a typically Parisian block of flats with half a dozen other people, including a member of the Lyne group. Gurdjieff's flat reminded Walker of a junk shop, with a remarkable mixture of furniture and a cozy haphazardness. 'Everything seemed to have happened by accident, and nothing by design.' It smelt of Eastern spices. Together with a large crowd, Walker and his wife entered a 'reading room' as oddly furnished as the hall, and for an hour listened to a pupil reading from a typescript of *Beelzebub*. Then Gurdjieff slipped quietly into the room – a short, stout man with a sweeping – and greying – moustache and piercing eyes. When Walker looked more closely, he saw that the eyes were friendly. Gurdjieff reminded him of old Chinese paintings of 'the Rogue'. After another hour of reading, Gurdjieff spoke. Rubbing his stomach, he announced that 'le patron' required feeding. They were all invited to lunch.

The huge crowd squeezed into the dining-room, where Gurdjieff was already seated on a divan with one foot tucked under the opposite knee. He proceeded to make a salad for his guests, with cucumber, pickles, red peppers, onions and sour cream. Then glasses were filled with Armagnac or vodka, and a pupil who had been appointed director proposed a toast. Walker (who was basically teetotal) had to take a great swig of vodka.

Gurdjieff he found impressive, with his vast, clean-shaven head and olive complexion. He claimed to be over 80 (although he was, in fact, 71), and he made Walker think of Haroun Al Raschid. Gurdjieff had been involved in another serious car accident earlier that year, but he showed no sign of it. The guests went on to eat pigeons stewed in vine leaves, pilaff, wild strawberries with cream, avocados, Turkish delight and melons. Meanwhile they had to drink endless toasts until Walker found the room expanding and contracting. This was Gurdjieff's method of getting to know people quickly and discovering their 'essence' – if they had any. When it was all over, he invited them all to dinner that evening.

Outside, Walker asked Mary what she thought of Gurdjieff.

'He's the most astonishing man I ever met. The chief impression he gave me was of immense vigour and of concentrated strength. I had the feeling that he was not really a man but a magician.' The Walkers went back to the hotel to sleep off the vodka. The evening meal was to be just as lavish, and would go on until after midnight.

Walker reached the interesting conclusion that Gurdjieff was trying to 'loosen up' the London disciples. Too much conscious self-discipline had made them rigid and grim. After Ouspensky, Gurdjieff must have seemed a salutary shock. The more Walker saw of Gurdjieff, the more he experienced a sense of freedom. Gurdjieff seemed to demonstrate by personal example that man's business is to be god-like.

Beelzebub struck Walker as badly written. But no sooner had he reached the conclusion that Gurdjieff was an unskilled writer than *Meetings with Remarkable Men* forced him to revise his opinion. His attempts to resolve these – and other – contradictions led him to conclude that Gurdjieff *intended* to create conflict and confusion. It was his way of teaching.

The lunches and dinners continued daily until Walker left. When he went to say goodbye, Gurdjieff told him to henceforth regard this flat as his own home, and offered to send him a regular supply of vodka to England. Walker was surprised by the rush of affection he felt as he shook hands.

That year Gurdjieff returned to America once more, and took over Ouspensky's New York group. There he made much the same kind of impact that he made on Walker in Paris – it is described by Irmis B. Popoff in her book *Gurdjieff* – and gave the same kind of vast and interminable meals.

But when Walker saw Gurdjieff in Paris again the following spring, he could see that his health was failing – undoubtedly under the burden of vast quantities of rich food and strong liquor. His breathing was laboured and his lips had a blue tinge. Walker diagnosed fluid in the abdomen and advised an operation to get rid of it. Gurdjieff thanked him, but said he was awaiting the arrival of a new drug from America.

Bennett, who now ran his own teaching group at Combe Springs in Surrey, also spent much time with Gurdjieff in

Paris. Gurdjieff's telepathic powers seemed to be unimpaired, and one morning, in a café, he dictated to Bennett an advertisement for the forthcoming edition of *Beelzebub* without opening his mouth. On Saturday 22 October, Bennett found him sitting in a café looking ill and tired, but Gurdjieff nevertheless made comments that indicated that he expected to live for at least another five years.

When the American doctor arrived four days later, however, he immediately ordered Gurdjieff to be removed to the American Hospital. His blood pressure was so high that it was impossible to inject serum. The liquid was finally drained from his stomach, but it had been left too late. On 29 October, 1949, Gurdjieff died. The autopsy revealed that he had been keeping himself alive by sheer will-power and vitality; the state of his inner organs was so bad that he should have died years earlier. Gurdjieff was an excellent advertisement for his own belief that a man lives by his powers of concentration.

1. I have discussed this, and Collin's other ideas, at some length in *Mysteries*.
2. My book on Gurdjieff, *The War Against Sleep*, contains a fuller account of his final years.

Seven

What Went Wrong?

CLEARLY, SOMETHING went wrong – both for Ouspensky and Gurdjieff. Ouspensky drank himself to death; Gurdjieff ate and drank himself to death. And although Gurdjieff's end was less anticlimactic than Ouspensky's, photographs taken during his last years confirm the impression of visitors who came to see him from England and America: that there was a touch of sadness about him.

In the case of Ouspensky, the question of what went wrong is easier to answer. Mystical experiences like the one on the Sea of Marmora confirmed his feeling that man could achieve a higher level of consciousness – that there is something essentially *false* about our everyday consciousness. As a man with training in science and mathematics, he shared the feeling of his contemporaries that man can rise 'on stepping stones of his dead selves to higher things'. His experiments with nitrous oxide seemed to support this. They confirmed beyond all doubt that 'higher consciousness' existed, and could, to some extent, be summoned at will. But Ouspensky's travels in the East were a disappointment; he failed to find what he was looking for.

Then he met Gurdjieff and became convinced that he was a man who 'knew'. And what Gurdjieff had to teach struck Ouspensky as appallingly true. The so-called 'individual' is not one self, but hundreds. His state of consciousness is actually a state of hypnotic sleep. He is virtually a machine. If he wishes to escape these limitations, it must be done by constant self-observation, by self-remembering, and by 'super-effort' or 'intentional suffering'.

It sounds as if all this is an excellent foundation on which to build a deliberate assault on the bastions of higher consciousness. Then what went wrong?

In order to grasp this, we must glance briefly at the history of the quest for 'higher consciousness' in the past two and a half centuries. From the point of view of man's intellectual evolution, the invention of the novel in the mid-eighteenth century is of inestimable importance. Samuel Richardson's *Pamela* (1740), a novel about the attempted seduction of a servant girl, taught men to daydream. Within a year or so, Europe had become 'a nation of readers'. Novels were a magic carpet that carried you away into other people's lives. Vast numbers of men and women – particularly women – who had accepted the boredom of their everyday lives and devoted their spare time to sewing cushion covers, now plunged into the exciting worlds of Rousseau, Goethe, Horace Walpole, 'Monk' Lewis, Mrs Radcliffe – worlds of romance, adultery, seduction and rape.

Goethe, whose novel *The Sorrows of Young Werther* (1774) had been immensely influential (even causing an epidemic of suicides), was also aware of something that earlier writers had scarcely noticed: the beauties of nature. Mountains and forests and lakes became part of the new 'romantic' consciousness. In England, Wordsworth and Coleridge – and then Byron and Shelley – followed his example. Wordsworth had been experiencing 'mystical' states since childhood. So had William Blake. It is in Blake that we can see most clearly the danger of this new romantic consciousness. In 'The Land of Dreams' the child asks his widowed father:

> 'Father, O Father! what do we here
> 'In this land of unbelief and fear?
> 'The Land of Dreams is better far,
> 'Above the light of the Morning Star.'

This rejection of the 'real world' and preference for the Land of Dreams is a highly dangerous state of mind, which leads to defeat and despair. And this was the major problem for all those poets, novelists and musicians who wanted their work to reflect the 'higher reality' of the Land of Dreams. They found reality too much for them, and died in droves.

By the end of the century – when Ouspensky was a young man – so many of these 'Outsider' artists had died young or committed suicide or gone mad that it became part of the romantic mythology that if you were a 'sensitive plant' you were virtually inviting an early death. Thomas Mann wrote novels in which death and intellectuality are always linked together, while Hermann Hesse's heroes go in search of 'higher consciousness', only to end by recognizing that it is not to be found in this 'land of unbelief and fear'.

In spite of his scientific temperament, Ouspensky was cast in the mould of a Hesse hero. He made the 'journey to the East' and returned empty-handed. He tried 'experimental mysticism' with the aid of dental gas, but found himself overwhelmed by romantic agony as he had to return to this 'wooden world', grinding on like some creaking mill. Then Gurdjieff held out new hope. Sheer *effort* could keep at bay the moods of romantic despair or the 'triviality of everydayness'. Practising self-remembering, Ouspensky found that he could wander around St Petersburg at night and sense the history of the houses as if they were living beings. He was able to induce moods of self-remembering in which he actually saw other people as sleepwalkers surrounded by their dreams. And on one occasion, he seemed on the point of breaking through to a new level of freedom before someone walked into the room and interrupted him. Gurdjieff's ability to communicate with him telepathically demonstrated that Gurdjieff had achieved certain 'magical' powers. This was also Ouspensky's aim.

What was self-evident was that the human mind has the power to 'hold' far higher levels of vital energy than are called upon in our everyday lives. If we could actually reach a high enough level of vitality and optimism, it would be so powerful that it would effect a kind of alchemical transformation of our inner being, a process of 'fusing'. But every time we begin to approach this level, we 'leak' and allow the energy to escape. Ouspensky could see that if he could learn to close those inner 'valves' that permit the energy to leak away, he could raise himself permanently to a higher level.

But he needed peace and security. Instead, he was uprooted and forced to become a wanderer in foreign lands. It was a traumatic experience for a gentle romantic. Fortunately, fate came to his rescue by making the West aware of *Tertium Organum*. He was welcomed in London; he became a celebrity. The story should now have had a happy ending. Unfortunately, Ouspensky's own temperament was the major obstacle to this. He had drunk deeply of the pessimistic aspects of Gurdjieff's doctrine: human beings are hopelessly self-divided; they are hypnotized sheep waiting for the butcher's knife. There can be no doubt that Ouspensky would have been a happier man if, instead of meeting Gurdjieff, he had met Rudolf Steiner, the Austrian mystic. Steiner would have taught him that the 'spirit world' lies inside us, and that we are all capable of 'access to higher worlds'. In fact, Gurdjieff had on Ouspensky much the same effect that the gloomy Schopenhauer had on Nietzsche: he gave his thinking an overwhelmingly pessimistic tinge. In *The Psychology of Man's Possible Evolution*, the first book in which Ouspensky tried to express what he had learned from Gurdjieff, all the emphasis is on human weakness and on man's inability to 'do'.

Gurdjieff himself was slightly better off, but not much. He had, in fact, seen the true solution to the problem that had killed off so many romantic Outsiders. The more we feel that the world is a 'land of unbelief and fear' or a 'dim vast vale of tears' or a 'misty dream', the more we are predisposed to run away from it. And this attitude puts us into a state of 'negative feedback': that is, our negative expectations cause us to 'leak', and the leakage confirms our pessimism by making it seem self-evident that life is a bore.

Gurdjieff had discovered that willed effort can close our inner leaks and raise our inner pressure. But in order to truly reverse the negative feedback process, a man would need to be driven by a certain optimism, a sense of what G.K.

Chesterton called 'absurd good news'; in other words, he would need to feel that such an effort is worthwhile. But here Gurdjieff's position was closer to that of Ouspensky. He was basically concerned – one might say obsessed – by what is *wrong* with people. His notion of the organ Kundabuffer, implanted in human beings to make them see illusion as reality, was a form of the legend of Original Sin. In his earliest piece of writing, *Herald of Coming Good*, he defines his original purpose as an attempt to prevent in himself the manifestations of 'Tzvarnoharno', something caused by the evil actions of common people, which leads to the destruction of those who would benefit humanity. And *Beelzebub's Tales to his Grandson* is an attempt to make people see what is wrong with them. The aim, according to Bennett, is to arouse feeling rather than thought, to create inner conflict that will carry readers beyond their intellectual processes.

Stanley Nott was convinced that this was what was wrong with Ouspensky. He wanted to turn Gurdjieff's teaching into an intellectual system. But Gurdjieff is saying – rather like Bergson – that intellect always misses the point, and that real understanding involves somehow 'shaking the mind awake'.

This is true – as far as it goes. But in trying to shake people out of old habits through inner conflict and 'intentional suffering', Gurdjieff was also missing the point.

The basic point is fairly simple. In those positive moods that Wordsworth describes in the 'Intimations of Immortality' ode, moods when the earth seems 'apparelled in celestial light', we experience an extremely clear and powerful sense that the world is a wonderful and fascinating place, and that we should be extremely grateful to be alive. We can *see* that it is marvellously rich and complex. But in order to perceive this, we need to be in a state of bubbling vitality. And our main problem is that our vitality leaks away too easily, leaving us too tired to appreciate this fascinating complexity – just as it is hard to read philosophy when you are tired.

Abraham Maslow tells a story of a marine who had been in the Pacific without seeing a woman, and, when he returned to base, saw a nurse and instantly had a 'peak experience' –

because he suddenly realized with tremendous force that *women are different from men*. This is 'newness' (Browning captures it in his phrase: 'How strange it seems, and new', and Ezra Pound meant the same thing when he called one of his books *Make It New*). Newness is the *recognition of difference*: that what you thought was 'the same' is not the same at all. What a poet sees on a spring morning is 'difference'. But as we grow tired – or discouraged – our senses smooth out the difference into sameness.

In fact this is really the basic problem of human existence. Habit causes us to 'silt up' like a river, until what was once narrow and fast becomes meandering and slow. This is what Wordsworth means when he complains that 'shades of the prison house' begin to close on us as we get older. Wordsworth's early poems – for example, the sonnet on Westminster Bridge – are full of 'newness', while the later poems are somehow 'tired'.

But we have already noted Maslow's important discovery that when he talked to his students about 'peak experiences', they began remembering peak experiences they had previously forgotten about. And as they began talking to one another about peak experiences, *they began having peak experiences all the time*.

The reason is obvious. The peak experience is a perception of difference. You look at some 'familiar' object and see it as new and strange. And you know that this perception is genuine, not some illusion. In fact, Ouspensky had grasped this vital insight in the passage about the factory chimneys in *Tertium Organum* (see p.33).

This is the 'spring morning' feeling. You *see* that everything is much stranger and more complex than your normal perception reveals. And you see that this *is* so. Like Maslow's marine, you are perceiving a real 'difference'. This is why people who have had peak experiences can go on repeating them: because it is simply a matter of *reminding yourself* of something you have already seen and which you know to be real. In this sense, it is like any other 'recognition' that suddenly dawns on you – for example, the recognition of the greatness of some composer or artist whom you had formerly found difficult or incomprehensible; or the recognition of how to solve a certain problem. Once such a recognition 'dawns', it is easy to re-establish contact with it, because it is there, like some possession, waiting for you to return to it.

Unfortunately, Ouspensky was not in a position to take advantage of this simple 'law of consciousness', because his basic assumptions were negative. So all his emphasis on self-remembering, self-observation, super-effort, was no more effective than his wife's altogether vaguer notions about the importance of religious insights. Whenever he felt tired, he was back to square one. And years of going back to square one finally convinced him that all his insights into human mechanicalness were useless, and that 'the System' had failed him.

He had failed to grasp a simple truth. If you feel tired but optimistic, a short rest will refresh you and re-charge your batteries. If you feel tired and pessimistic, even a sleep may leave you feeling as tired as ever.

Again, consider what happens when something goes wrong, and you put it right. 'Putting it right' has the effect of making you feel delighted that things are 'back to normal', and that 'normality' is a highly desirable state. Yet when things *are* normal, and have been normal for a long time, we take normality for granted; in fact, we may even find it boring. The act of 'putting something right' has the interesting effect of making you see 'normality' as delightful. In fact, it momentarily lifts you into a perception of 'newness', of 'difference', and once again raises you to the perception that reality is infinitely fascinating.

To recognize this is to recognize that our 'normal' perception has a strong pessimistic component, a kind of 'free-floating anxiety', making us aware of the truth of William James's observation that, for much of the time, we 'feel as if a sort of cloud weighed upon us, keeping us below our highest notch in clearness in discernment, sureness in reasoning, or firmness in deciding'.

Now this observation occurs in the essay called 'The

Energies of Man', which has been discussed earlier in this book, and which makes clear the point that Gurdjieff and James are talking about the same thing: 'second wind' or 'vital reserves'. It is also plain that we can break through to 'second wind' by a deliberate effort of will. James appears to be saying the same thing as Gurdjieff: that we *are* diseased, and that the disease is called Original Sin (or Kundabuffer). But there is an important difference. James recognizes that our negativity is a kind of 'cloud' weighing upon us. James was an optimistic kind of person and, like G.K. Chesterton, he recognized that the basis of reality is 'absurd good news'.

What all this amounts to is the recognition that both Gurdjieff and Ouspensky were inclined to make the same mistake: they over-emphasized the idea of super-effort or intentional suffering. Beyond a certain point, super-effort tends to be counterproductive: it produces fatigue and pessimism.

Consider what happens when you receive some good news, or some anticipated crisis evaporates. There is a sudden perception that the world is delightful. And this *transfers itself to your subconscious mind*, so that even an hour or so later, when you have forgotten about the crisis, you remain in a state of bubbling vitality, as if a kind of 'underfloor lighting' had been switched on. If we could train ourselves to keep the underfloor lighting switched on, our lives would become immensely satisfying and productive.

The odd thing is that every time we experience 'absurd good news', we see that it *is* an objective fact, and that consequently, there is no earthly reason why, with a little effort, it should not become a permanent state.

Does this mean that no effort is necessary? Clearly not. Our real problem is our inbuilt tendency to 'leak', to allow our inner pressure to sink unnoticed. In *The War Against Sleep* I expressed the problem in the sentence: 'Human beings are like grandfather clocks driven by watchsprings.' But the real trouble is lack of inner pressure – 'leakage'.

What prevents leakage? *Focusing the attention*. The Zen master Ikkyu was once asked by a workman to write something on his slate; Ikkyu wrote the word 'Attention.' The workman looked disappointed. 'Couldn't you write something else?' Ikkyu wrote: 'Attention, attention.' The workman asked: 'What does attention mean?', and Ikkyu replied: 'Attention means attention.'

He could have replied: 'Attention means focusing your energies and closing your leaks, so you are in a higher energy state.'

Leakage keeps us in a constant state of low inner pressure. But in order to do anything well, you require high inner pressure.

Some personal remarks on my own experience of 'the method' may clarify the point. I came upon Ouspensky's *In Search of the Miraculous* and Kenneth Walker's *Venture with Ideas* in 1951, when I was 20. They filled me with excitement. But at that time, I had already discovered the basic method for the control of consciousness. Like many teenagers, I had suffered a great deal from 'life failure', the feeling that life is meaningless and pointless, and that the efforts it demands of us are a waste of time. For a great deal of the time, my everyday life seemed grey and dull. I craved 'satisfaction', a higher quality of life, yet felt that this was a purely biological craving that did nothing to redeem life from meaninglessness. In fact, life seemed so meaningless that it seemed a waste of time even to kill myself. Eliot's *Hollow Men* seemed to me to express the basic truth about human existence. So did Auden's lines:

> Put the car away; when life fails
> What's the good of going to Wales?

But in an essay of T.S. Eliot I came upon a reference to the *Bhagavad Gita*, and when I came upon a new translation of it – by Isherwood – in the local bookshop, I bought it.

The *Gita* brought about a total change of attitude. To begin with, it persuaded me to sit cross-legged on the floor, focusing my attention. There were times when I concentrated so hard that I went red in the face. But I suddenly discovered, to my astonishment, that the sense of futility and greyness had vanished. The world suddenly became so interesting that I would often pause to look at a privet leaf, or at a cracked windowsill.

What had happened is obvious. Teenage depression had led to constant 'leakage' and negative feedback. Perception is 'intentional'; in order to perceive anything, you have to throw your attention at it like a javelin. The strength of my throwing arm had become so enfeebled that the javelin was falling at my feet, instead of impaling its object. Reading poetry and listening to music had alleviated the problem, but even if I achieved a state of total affirmation, it had vanished by the following day. Sitting cross-legged and concentrating taught me that it did not have to vanish.

At this point, life suddenly became more complicated. I married and became a father, and that meant I had no time for sitting cross-legged. By the time I came home from the factory, I was exhausted. So I ceased to 'meditate'.

Fortunately, this was the period when I came upon Gurdjieff and Ouspensky. *In Search of the Miraculous* was a tremendous mental stimulus. Reading it required less effort than concentrating, but it could restore that sense of high inner pressure, and restore my sense of purpose. And when, three years later, I wrote my first book, *The Outsider*, it was inevitable that Gurdjieff and Ouspensky should figure prominently.

I had no doubt then – and still have no doubt – that Gurdjieff was perhaps the greatest man of the twentieth century. I became a friend of Kenneth Walker, and what he told me confirmed that impression. Yet I never felt that Walker himself had achieved any high degree of self-discipline. And I continued to feel this in subsequent years when I met followers of Gurdjieff and Ouspensky. Bennett struck me as altogether more disciplined, yet oddly narrow. And I found it totally incomprehensible that he had turned from Gurdjieff to Pakh Subuh, and then became a Catholic convert. That seemed to demonstrate once and for all that, in spite of having read *Beelzebub* a dozen times, he still had no idea of what Gurdjieff was talking about. In retrospect, I am inclined to wonder whether, like Ouspensky, Bennett felt that the System had failed him.

Another Ouspensky disciple whom I came to like and admire – and who shall remain nameless – was not even sure of the difference between 'essence' and 'personality'; he thought personality was the 'true self' and essence the 'false self'.

Clearly, then, Gurdjieff had not succeeded in stamping his genius on any of his followers – with the exception of Ouspensky, who already possessed his own genius.

When I came to write *The War Against Sleep* – in 1979 – I tried hard to put my finger on what had gone wrong, particularly in the last chapter, 'Gurdjieff versus Ouspensky?' I saw Ouspensky's problem as his pessimism, and his failure to grasp the 'absurd good news' experience. And I accurately characterized Gurdjieff's problem as his overemphasis on super-effort. Yet although it seems to me that I have clearly stated 'what went wrong', I have not tried hard enough to state how it could have been put right.

Let me try again.

'Peak experiences' involve the sense of 'difference' and 'newness'. Most serious modern literature seems to be based on what I have called the 'fallacy of insignificance', the feeling that intelligent people are bound to be weak and neurotic, and that, as Yeats said, 'We have not begun to live until we have conceived of life as tragedy.' That, in short, 'you can't win'. The peak experience is a sudden overwhelming certainty that you *can* win.

In a book called *Beyond the Occult*, I have suggested that it is helpful to distinguish seven basis levels of human consciousness.

If we regard deep sleep as Level O, then Level 1 would be dreaming. Level 2 is the level you experience when you wake up in the middle of the night from a deep sleep: a kind of passive, disoriented consciousness. We also experience this when we are very tired, and we look at things without actually 'seeing' them. You could say there is no 'I' present.

Level 3 is the level at which 'I' emerges, but at which you still feel low and dull. I spent much of my teens in Level 3. Shaw called it 'life failure', and Camus 'the absurd'; it is the feeling that reality is quite meaningless in itself, and that *we* impose meanings on it.

Level 4 is our normal, everyday consciousness. And in the lower end of Level 4, life still seems appallingly hard work. Emily Brontë captures it in the poem that begins:

> Does the road wind uphill all the way?
> Right to the very end.

But about halfway up Level 4, we begin to experience an odd sense of strength and optimism, a feeling that obstacles *can* be overcome and that life can be delightful after all. At the top end of 'everyday consciousness', we feel oddly certain that 'you *can* win'.

Maslow's 'peak experience' – that sudden bubbling feeling of total happiness – might be regarded as a kind of spark that leaps the gap between Levels 4 and 5. Level 5 is what I have called 'spring morning consciousness', the perception of 'newness' and 'difference', the feeling that the world is infinitely fascinating after all.

Such feelings seldom last long. But when they do, they constitute virtually a new level of consciousness – what J.B. Priestley calls 'magic'. A child on Christmas Day may experience 'magic'; so may a couple on honeymoon. According to Yeats, it is the feeling Paris experienced in Helen's arms for the first time: 'What were all the world's alarms?' – a feeling that there is *no* problem that cannot be overcome.

Level 7 is what I have called 'Faculty X', that curious ability we experience in certain moments to grasp the reality of other times and places. Proust experienced it (and described it in *Swann's Way*) when he tasted a small cake dipped in herb tea and suddenly recalled, with tremendous clarity, his childhood in a French village. Arnold Toynbee described the feeling many times in his *Study of History*. In Faculty X, we seem to transcend time. If human beings could achieve

Faculty X, their whole lives would become as accessible to them as the past hour.

There is, in fact, a Level 8; Ouspensky experienced it with nitrous oxide. This is 'mystical' consciousness in which we become aware that everything in the universe is connected together.

If we ignore Level 8, and concentrate on the seven levels of ordinary consciousness, we see that our everyday consciousness, Level 4, is precisely halfway up the scale. Moreover, the level at which we begin to feel 'you *can* win' is precisely halfway up Level 4, at 3½. Of course, we may regard the seven levels as completely arbitrary – for example, if we included the so-called hypnogogic states on the verge of sleeping and waking, there could easily be eight levels – yet it is still of practical significance to consider Level 3½ as the 'halfway mark'. For we see that the lower levels are the levels in which we feel that life is futile and meaningless, or tragically difficult. When Sartre says: 'Man is a useless passion' he is merely stating the typical outlook of Level 3.

Up to Level 3½, life is uphill work. But beyond that, it becomes immensely exciting: the peak experience, spring morning consciousness, magic consciousness, Faculty X, mystical consciousness . . . And if we become clearly aware that what keeps us below Level 3½ is simply 'leakage', and the pessimism that comes from negative feedback – the tendency to feel gloomy because we *see* life as gloomy, so that disaster becomes a self-fulfilling prophecy – we can also glimpse a magnificent possibility: that there is no good reason why a few human beings should not 'close their inner valves', maintain a higher level of inner pressure, and remain *permanently* abo Level 3½. I have succeeded in doing it for days at a time, ar only regret the number of years I have wasted because I w unaware that it could be done.

Now interestingly enough, it is clear that Ouspensky final became disillusioned with the System because he sudden recognized this same possibility. When, during his last peri at Lyne, he told his pupils that they should have straightforward, everyday aim, and that only by workir alone can one make progress, he was recognizing that a life devoted to the System tends to become as narrow as a life devoted to daily attendance at church. As Walker observed, the London followers had become too rigid and grim. Maslow had also recognized that the people he called 'self-actualizers' have straightforward, everyday aims like other people, but they pour their heart and soul into these everyday aims. A self-actualizer does not have to be a Beethoven or a Michelangelo. It may be a man who takes enormous pleasure in putting ships in bottles or collecting stamps. Maslow cites a woman who was a marvellous mother and who, when she was too old to have more children, adopted children so she could do 'what she was good at'. To do *anything* with this kind of enthusiasm and conviction recharges our vital batteries. Hermann Hesse makes his narrator remark, in *Journey to the East*, 'I, whose calling was only that of a violinist and storyteller, was responsible for the provision of music for our group, and I then discovered how *a long time devoted to small details exalts us and increases our strength*' (my italics). It causes us to make contact with what Granville Barker calls 'the Secret Life', the wellsprings of vitality deep inside us. As we have seen, Maslow even cured a girl suffering from exhaustion and life failure by advising her to go to night school to study a subject that really interested her. As soon as we do anything with enthusiasm, with conviction, with total attention, life takes on a 'real' quality. Our greatest human mistake is to feel that certain things do not *deserve* enthusiastic attention. We have to learn that *anything* done with enthusiastic attention exalts us and increases our strength.

Now in fact, it is relatively easy to recharge our vital batteries. Let me suggest, for example, that if you have been sitting still for some time, reading this book, you bend your arms and tense your shoulder muscles, or simply yawn and stretch. Note the way that this causes a feeling of pleasure to ripple through your muscles. Next, try shutting your eyes very tight as you do it, and twisting up your face into a grimace. Again, you notice that odd 'ripple' of energy and pleasure. In fact, the face muscles play an important part in the control of energy, and this is one of the easiest methods of summoning a minor peak experience.

There are other methods – for example, concentrating intently on a pen help up against the ceiling, making a tremendous effort, then relaxing until you become aware of the whole wall, then concentrating again . . .

Gurdjieff once remarked that there is a vast reservoir of universal energy which is accessible to us, and that with the right kind of effort, we can place ourselves in touch with this energy. Anton Mesmer also believed that there are 'tides' of universal energy that sweep through our bodies, keeping us healthy. (Wilhelm Reich called it 'orgone energy'.) If we become 'blocked', we become unhealthy. But if you concentrate hard, using your face muscles, and bracing your arms, you can experience a sensation of *driving* the energies down through your body. If you continue to do this for a quarter of an hour or so – for example, on a train journey when you have nothing better to do – you begin to experience a curiously 'wide-awake' feeling, and everything you look at seems 'more interesting'.[1] It should be emphasized, in passing, that these exercises can be quite unobtrusive, so that fellow passengers would not even notice.

The most useful time of all, I have found, is the middle of the night, if I happen to be lying awake. It is important to recognize that our usual 'passive' consciousness is not a particularly desirable state, and that counting sheep is not necessarily the best way to utilize the mind. I find that, in the middle of the night, five minutes of 'concentration exercises' begin to produce active pleasure, as I feel the energy being driven down through my body. Sometimes the pleasure is so great that I want to stay awake. But half an hour or so of 'concentration' brings a pleasant tiredness, and I find that I then drift into sleep with a curious sense of happiness. Moreover, once I have achieved this odd sense of control over myself, it becomes possible to 'navigate' one's way into dreams – the phrase is obscure, but it is the best I can do – so that plunging into sleep has a controlled quality, like diving into a pool; there are occasions when the sensation is so pleasant that I enjoy drifting in and out of sleep like someone being swept through the waves on a surfboard. I also observe that, after a night of this kind of sleep, I experience a high level of mental energy, and as I write, am aware that an act of sudden 'attention' can produce a flash of pure delight.

This seems to me to be one of the basic secrets. This deliberate control of energy makes me aware that consciousness was never intended to be passive, and that the solving of problems, which most of us regard as one of the more alarming aspects of life, can and should be a thoroughly enjoyable activity. But we are too passive. We fail to realize that when we experience a 'sinking feeling' of boredom or depression, this has nothing to do with external reality; it is a kind of confidence trick played on us by our 'robot'. It is due, quite simply, to lack of inner pressure, lack of energy. The water has been allowed to sink too low in the well, and it takes a great many strokes on the pump to bring it to the surface. But the act of concentrating, of driving the energies through the body, brings these energies to the surface, and life is suddenly fascinating and meaningful again.

In short, we allow the robot to get away with far too much. That is the essence of Gurdjieff's message.

What seems absurd is that Ouspensky failed to grasp that he was applying his remarkable will-power *in the wrong direction*. He was like a man trying to push open a door that opens the other way. 'Experimental Mysticism' is the fullest description of Level 8 on record. And Ouspensky's central recognition in this state is that *everything in the universe is connected* – which, in turn, is Chesterton's 'absurd good news'. Our 'normal' consciousness divides things. It is like a narrow flashlight beam that plays over objects in a darkened room, but can never illuminate the room as a whole. This means that human beings suffer from a kind of permanent 'tunnel vision', a 'certain blindness'. The most extreme form of this tunnel vision is when we are very tired and depressed (it might be a good idea to substitute the word 'depressurized', for this makes the nature of the problem more obvious), and things around us look somehow meaningless, 'merely themselves'. This is Level 3, what Sartre called 'nausea', and it makes an extraordinary impression of truth and authenticity. Yet it is rather like believing that a picture gallery in the dark has no pictures in it. The moment our inner pressure carries us up to Level 3½, we become aware that we can *choose* between these two views: 'nausea' and meaning.

Our problem is that as soon as we allow ourselves to become 'depressurized', the meaning vanishes and 'nausea' seems to be the only reality. When children experience such states, they are defenceless. Adults, fortunately, have a line of defence: the intellect. Many Victorians had a remarkable grasp of this insight, and Matthew Arnold expressed it in a poem called 'Morality':

> We cannot kindle when we will
> The fire which in the heart resides.
> The spirit bloweth and is still;
> In mystery our soul abides;
> But tasks in hours of insight willed
> Can be through hours of gloom fulfilled.

Once a poet has actually *seen* this meaning he can, with a certain amount of stubbornness and intellectual toughness, hang on to it. It could be compared to navigating in a fog with a compass rather than by the stars.

The man who stands the best chance of fighting his way back into the state of insight is the one who has the best memory for the stars. And a man who has seen the stars a dozen times will obviously have a better memory for them than a man who has only seen them once or twice. And a man who has seen them hundreds of times can never forget them or doubt their existence. This is why we attach such immense importance to these states of 'wider consciousness', and will purchase them at high cost to our health, or even to our lives. The artist or poet who chooses poverty and 'outsiderism' to comfort and security is an example. So is the monk and the yogi. So, unfortunately, is the alcoholic and drug addict and rapist.

Ouspensky's repeated experience of Level 8 – described in 'Experimental Mysticism' – should have provided him with a very good working knowledge of the stars. The recognition that 'everything is connected' is a recognition that there is an 'overall meaning', and that it should therefore be possible for man to achieve it. Ouspensky had an obscure sense that it was somehow wrong to use nitrous oxide to obtain this knowledge, and he was correct. You could say that he had used a balloon to get to heaven when he should have been building a ladder – a ladder of words and concepts – that others could have used after him. Moreover, he had not sufficiently strengthened his sense of reality to be able to cope with the 'landing'. Instead of feeling that everyday reality *contains* all these hidden meanings, these immense vistas of 'connectedness', he could only groan with anguish, like a child who wants Christmas to go on forever. This was the price that he paid for his 'short cut'.

When Ouspensky discovered Gurdjieff, though, it seemed that now, at last, he had his 'ladder', a means of achieving higher states of consciousness through ordinary conscious effort. His certainty that he had stumbled upon a completely new approach to the problem of higher consciousness was increased by some of Gurdjieff's odder and more paradoxical ideas – such as that knowledge is 'material', and therefore cannot be shared out indefinitely, or that human beings are 'food of the moon'. After his 'short cut' with nitrous oxide, he now went to the opposite extreme, and became entrenched in a kind of gleeful pragmatism. His total refusal to countenance anything that sounded like 'mysticism' has something in common with Marx's view that religion is the opium of the people. In effect, Ouspensky had become a kind of 'spiritual Marxist'. This attitude certainly made an immense impact on his followers in London, and later in America, producing the impression that he had *the* answer. In effect, he ordered everyone to toe the party line or else . . . Yet this attitude was the reverse of what he had stood for in *Tertium Organum* and *A New Model of the Universe*. It seems incredible that this 'Marxist' Ouspensky could have allowed himself to publish the chapter on Notre Dame, the Pyramids and the Sphinx, which sound as if they have been written by some disciple of Madame Blavatsky.

Significantly, of course, Gurdjieff himself was anything but a 'spiritual Marxist'. His approach remained fundamentally religious. This was the basic reason why Ouspensky had to renounce him. Ouspensky felt that he had taken Gurdjieff's System and discarded the nonsense. Religion and mysticism were traps for the woolly-minded. He had no time for such 'opium'.

Yet by the time he went to America, it had become clear to Ouspensky that his own 'Marxianized' version of the System was getting him nowhere. It left him trapped in 'tunnel vision' and only strong alcohol could enable him to 'open up'. Gurdjieff never made the same mistake: he ate, drank, fornicated and prayed, and remained a well-rounded human being. If we are to believe *Beelzebub*, the only thing he lacked was that deep, Chestertonian conviction of 'absurd good news'.

When Madame Ouspensky began to encourage the study of religious texts, Ouspensky allowed her to do so, for he was now aware of the shortcomings of his own approach. Yet this was a total reversal of what he had believed when he came to England in 1921, when such dilution of the System would have been harshly treated. And finally, as Nott has recorded, he felt like abandoning the System altogether and going off once more in search of 'secret doctrines' and hidden knowledge. His attempt to 'Marxianize' the System had left him intellectually bankrupt.

According to disciples who were with him in the last months of his life, Ouspensky achieved peace at the end. The 'tunnel vision' disappeared as death approached, and he probably felt that his attempt to intellectualize the System had not been such a waste of time after all. At least it had produced a masterpiece, in his record of his years with Gurdjieff, a book in which all his early clarity, brilliance and honesty combined to produce the perfect introduction to Gurdjieff's ideas. Without *In Search of the Miraculous*, 'the war against sleep' would certainly have made very little headway in the twentieth century, which has no time to get to grips with a work like *Beelzebub's Tales*. Half a century later, Ouspensky's book remains by far the best introduction to Gurdjieff.

It is a pity that Ouspensky never produced such an excellent introduction to Ouspensky. *Tertium Organum* and *A New Model of the Universe* both strike us as an odd mixture of brilliance and confusion. But if he had never written anything else, they would make us aware that Ouspensky was a powerful and original mind, comparable to Soloviev, Rozanov, Berdyaev and other major Russian thinkers. Instead posterity will continue to regard him as another man's interpreter.

Still, if the accounts of the serenity of his final days are accurate, it may be that this is how he would have preferred to be remembered.

1. I have described two such occasions at length in *Beyond the Occult*, Chapter 2.

Index

Anyone who has enjoyed this book, and wishes to learn more about Colin Wilson, might be interested in ABRAXAS, a magazine containing stories, poems and articles by established and new writers, as well as book reviews and essays by Wilson himself. It also offers a special service whereby readers can receive personally signed copies of his books. Further details can be obtained by writing to:

ABRAXAS,
57 Eastbourne Road,
St Austell,
Cornwall,
PL25 4SU.